# Praise for
## Retaking America: Crushing Political Correctness

"Sometimes it takes someone who grew up outside of America to remind us just how exceptional a nation we were blessed to be born in. Nick Adams makes a distinctive, fresh, provocative and insightful argument for more American leadership in a changing world."
- Dana Perino, former White House Press Secretary and *New York Times* bestselling author of *And the Good News Is . . .*

"He recognizes that the source of American exceptionalism is the people and not the government."
- Ben Carson, MD, bestselling author of *One Nation: What We Can All Do to Save America's Future*

"Explosive, devastating and at times, laugh-out-loud hilarious, Adams provides an acute, eye-opening and inspiring analysis . . . The young Australian may not be politically correct, but he's closer to dead-on accurate than 95% of the voices you have heard in the past many years."
- Hugh Hewitt, host of nationally syndicated radio show *The Hugh Hewitt Show*

"Nick Adams is back, more fearless than ever . . . *Retaking America* is candid, funny, bold and compulsory reading . . . a rousing manifesto against liberal thuggery . . . it's a terrific page-turner."
- Lt Col Oliver North, USMC (Ret), Fox News

"Leave it to the Australian to make one of the most revealing and incisive analyses of American political correctness . . . Nick Adams makes a passionate and compelling case against the growth of an overly PC culture, and does so with a clever wit."
- Doug Brunt, *New York Times* bestselling author of *The Means* and *Ghosts of Manhattan*

"Political correctness has a big mouth, and Nick Adams fills it with a well-deserved knuckle sandwich . . . *Retaking America* an unvarnished lo-down from Down Under . . . Adams once again provides a terrific read that tells the Left in plain and simple Aussie where it can stick its tucker bag."
- *National Review*

"A must-read!"
- Dick Morris, bestselling author of *Power Grab*, former adviser to President Bill Clinton

"Nick Adams—the de Tocqueville traveler of our times—has captured the essence of why America is destined to remain great."
- Edwin J. Feulner, Ph.D, founder and former president of the Heritage Foundation

". . . an ode to individuality as well as a great game plan . . . "
- *NRA News*

"Every time Adams says 'God Bless America,' we should think to ourselves: 'God Bless Australia – for sending us Nick Adams.'"
- *World Magazine*

". . . a provocative and impassioned defense of the American idea, and a clarion call to abolish political correctness . . "
- *The Blaze*

"Adams' conservative insight is invaluable and irresistible."
- Ben Shapiro, Editor-at-Large, Breitbart.com

". . . a powerful pep talk for Team USA . . . the kind of bracing, snap-out-of-it, kick-in-the-pants that a great nation needs . . ."
- Jack Fowler, publisher of *National Review*

"Adams is an eloquent voice for conservatism, bringing intelligence and optimism about America's future."
- *Dartmouth Review*

*"Give me your tired, your poor, your huddled masses yearning to breathe free."*

Emma Lazarus, "New Colossus"
(also known as "The Statue of Liberty Poem")

To the American people:
the most optimistic, patriotic, individualistic,
religious, enterprising, charitable, innovative, competitive,
inspirational, principled, confident, and courageous
people I have ever encountered.

# CONTENTS

Prologue .................................................................... ix

Introduction ............................................................... xi

Build A Wall? The Left Already Has One ....................... 1

Epilogue ................................................................... 75

Supporting FLAG ...................................................... 85

Acknowledgements .................................................... 91

About the Author ....................................................... 93

A POST HILL PRESS BOOK
ISBN: 978-1-68261-305-4
ISBN (eBook): 978-1-68261-306-1

Green Card Warrior:
My Quest for Legal Immigration in an Illegals' System
© 2016 by Nick Adams
All Rights Reserved

Cover Design by Quincy Alivio

**Post Hill**
PRESS

Post Hill Press
posthillpress.com

Published in the United States of America

# GREEN CARD
# WARRIOR

# NICK ADAMS

# PROLOGUE

It's December 1985 in Sydney, Australia.

Two parents are at wits' end. Something is not right with their 16-month-old child. For months, they have visited doctor after doctor. No one can tell them what is wrong. On the night before Christmas Eve, with their child more unsettled than usual, they head for the emergency room at the Children's Hospital.

The ward is nearly deserted, but there is one overnight doctor—a young man with a smiling face and an accent. As he looks the child over, the smile evaporates: "I think your son has Neuroblastoma. Get him in for tests first thing in the morning." The next day, the parents' worst fears would be confirmed. It was Stage IV Neuroblastoma, a rare type of childhood cancer.

The parents were mine. The child was me. The doctor, it turned out, was an American.

The cause of Neuroblastoma remains unknown today. Only 1 in 100,000 children get it. Notoriously difficult to diagnose, by the time it is, the tumor has usually spread. At Stage IV, an infant has just a five percent chance of life—only one in twenty survive. For three years, I underwent chemotherapy, radiotherapy, and an operation.

Through the healing hands of God, the master physician, I defied the odds, and lived. The instincts of the American doctor, fresh out of college, only in Australia for an internship, just in time, were crucial.

So I haven't only studied American exceptionalism.

I've lived it.

In fact, I'm alive because of it.

# INTRODUCTION

I was born burning for America.

I'm reliably told the first word to ever leave my mouth was "Coke"—as in Coca Cola, a sign of the capitalist and American disciple I would become!

As young as eight, I told my parents and teachers I wanted to go to America to speak to people. They thought I was crazy.

You must understand: I am of Greek and German descent, born in Australia. No one in my family had even visited America before me.

Interestingly, my paternal grandfather had a choice between immigrating to America or Australia in the early 1950s, but chose Australia since his older brother had already made the journey. How different would my life have been had the coin landed the other way! This book would certainly never have been written.

My parents were always pro-American. I was raised to believe America was a force for good in the world, and that it should take its leadership role seriously, because an absent America meant a dangerous world.

I turned seventeen on September 5, 2001. As I watched the World Trade Center towers tumble down six days later, I knew it was the responsibility of my generation to stand up and protect America and Western civilization.

I was the Valedictorian at school. I was publicly elected to political office at the age of nineteen I was the youngest Deputy Mayor in Australian history at twenty-one.

By the time I was twenty-five, I realized I was an American trapped in an Australian body, and was desperate to get out. At that age, with undergraduate and postgraduate degrees from the University of Sydney in my pocket, I decided it was finally time to travel to visit the country to whose freedom I had been captive for so long.

I was excited by its flair. Attracted by its opportunity. Inspired by its story. Captured by its hope.

The war on America is real. Anti-Americanism worldwide is on the rise. Political correctness is out of control. While decline is a choice, and not a condition, the America we know and love is slipping.

But despite this, it's important not to overlook America's treasure.

I have only ever known American soil during President Obama's time in office, and still almost every one of my dreams and ambition materialized. In just a few short years, I'd achieved more than I ever had, or could have, in my own country. I became a best-selling author before the age of thirty.

Many of you may wonder why immigrating to America was necessary at all.

Australia once offered a version of the American dream, but that no longer exists. It is hidden by the symbols of political correctness: big government, gatekeepers, envy, an aversion to risk, and collectivism. When the focus is on the collective, individual dreams can never fully materialize.

The international perception of Australia and the domestic reality are worlds apart. It may surprise many of you, but Australia is one of the most politically correct countries in the world. It's not the U.K., but it's not far behind.

For as long as I can remember, the bureaucracy has insisted that people dealing with government departments (e.g. universities, hospitals, employment services, and so forth) be asked if they identify themselves as Aboriginal, or if English were their first language. Not surprisingly, more Australians are choosing to identify themselves as Aboriginal as ever before, as it is advantageous for affirmative action and victim status.

Generally speaking, Australians worship rules, dislike risk, and love structure. They have faith in government, and a reverence for bureaucrats. They are guarded, and there is a discernible lack of optimism in the culture. Given the choice between a leader who conforms to the consensus, and a leader who creates consensus to their own vision and goals, Australians will always choose the former. This is a result of Australians elevating "feeling comfortable" over being the best they can be. By comfort, I mean a safety net, which includes unlimited unemployment benefits, unlimited health care, and a raft of social security measures that would make a Soviet planner blush.

In Australia, the control and power of the political and media establishment is far more influential than America's. "Gatekeepers" exist at every turn in these fields, and if you judge the absence of any substantial objection in the community to their presence, one can only conclude that these establishment gatekeepers enjoy the support of the Australian people.

This is not new.

You have probably heard of the Sydney Opera House. It is the international icon of Australia, instantly recognized worldwide. But the story of its construction is not so well known. The masterpiece was the brainchild of award-winning Danish architect Jørn Utzon. He loved Sydney passionately, with visions of it becoming the international city it became. He worked on the Opera House for nine years, completing the concrete shells of the exterior, easily the most difficult part of the structure. But he was forced to leave the project before its completion, after repeated badgering from government officials over design, fees, materials, and costs. Such was his treatment (creativity stifled, boldness resented) and so underappreciated did he feel, he left Australia in 1966, vowing never to return.

Utzon kept his word. Until the day he died in 2008, he never returned, declining several invitations.

It shouldn't surprise Americans that the majority of the famous Australians with whom they are familiar choose to live in the United States, rather than in their own country.

None of this is to defame Australia.

It is a lucky country. It is a great country. I still love it. I'm proud of Australia's history, particularly its record as a long-time ally of America.

But I know that Australia is not America, and that my country has not achieved what America has achieved. No country in human history has.

How could it? America is much more than a country. It's an ideal, a value system. Put simply, it's the best idea the world has ever had. That's why American greatness and leadership is indispensable to civilization, as we know it.

It's why I have dedicated my life to ensuring America remains the different place it has always been. It's why I have sought to restore American confidence.

America is the shot that was heard around the world, and still is. It's the experiment that was launched and still breathes. It's the improbable and daring idea that remains just as improbable and daring today.

It's the hope that banishes hopelessness.

Politically and culturally, I've always been a conservative.

I believe in in the traditional family, God, personal responsibility, the sanctity of human life, patriotism, self-reliance, individual liberty, limited government, the right to bear arms, free markets, the state of Israel, a strong national defense, and that welfare should be largely a family and church responsibility.

But more than any of those things—I believe in America.

What you are about to read provided a serious test of not just my Christian charity, but also that very belief.

It was written as a diary/journal, often in the moment, sometimes days after the described event.

# BUILD A WALL?
## THE LEFT ALREADY HAS ONE

It's October 19, 2015.

My life is falling apart.

I look over to the calendar, hanging near my desk. October 8 is the date circled on my calendar. It was the day I had dreamed about for years. It was to be the end of the most painstaking and expensive process of my life. It had taken close to four years and thirty-five thousand dollars to get here.

It was meant to be the day I immigrated to the greatest country of them all: America. My Qantas flight was booked and fully paid for. My events were lined up. People were expecting me. It would have been my sixteenth trip to America.

Instead, I am still in Australia, with no passport, and facing the very real prospect of already having set foot for the very last time on American soil.

My heart is breaking.

★

Ten months ago, it couldn't have been more different.

It was December 30, 2014. I'll never forget the date. Summer time. The sun is pouring in. My mother is already at work. My father, a school teacher, is on school holidays. I stumble out of bed, and into my bathroom, proceeding to rub the sleep out of my eyes by splashing cold water on my face.

Towelling off briefly, I head to the corner of my bedroom where my Blackberry has charged overnight. I check my phone for emails, my daily morning ritual.

There was an email from my immigration attorney. I opened it. It read:

*Wonderful news (and a belated Christmas present)! Please see the attached approval notice of your immigrant visa petition.*

I'd done it. Finally. The United States Citizenship and Immigration Service had approved my Extraordinary Ability Green Card petition.

My heart smiled.

I was going to be an American.

★

For as long as I can remember, I wanted to be an American.

As young as eight, I started to tell my parents, teachers and anybody that would listen that I wanted to go to America. Don't ask me why. It was just so. America has that effect on some people. Some of us are just born burning for America. We can't wait to get there.

We see opportunity, dreams, and greatness. We see fewer gatekeepers and observe how a little creativity and risk goes so much further than in our own countries. It's a chance to fail. We're intoxicated by the freedom and individuality that give America its color and vibrancy. We're magnetized by the relentless optimism and palpable energy that Americans don't even know they have.

★

But getting to America the right way is hard.

Those born in America win the lottery of life. Those that aren't, but want or need to come, are in for the fight of their life.

It is often said that the immigration system is "broken." But that doesn't even begin to describe it. It's more than broken. It's an unmitigated disaster. A train wreck. A car crash. A frustrating, unfair disgrace to America's founding principles and her enduring values. It is a bureaucratic process that completely contradicts the American way. It is a contrast so stark to the kind and generous character of everyday Americans that it is tantamount to libel.

This "broken" system breaks families, finances, and fortitude. It snaps sanity and slays the soul.

The tragic part is it has been this way for as long as anyone can remember. And apart from a little self-serving lip-service every now and again, no one does anything about it. There is no will to fix it.

Never once through this have I considered coming to America illegally.

I love America, and the last thing I would entertain is breaking the law of the country I love and seek to adopt as my own.

No country should want somebody who feels otherwise.

But I must tell you, my life would be much easier if I were so inclined.

I speak, write, and appear as a conservative commentator to make a living. It's not easy, but it is what I love.

I am best known for my work in the field of American exceptionalism.

Recently, I began the process of setting up my own 501(c)(3) non-profit, called the *Foundation for Liberty and American*

*Greatness*, or FLAG. It aims to promote patriotic principles and diminish anti-Americanism.

For the last five years, I have been one of the world's longest distance commuters, traveling between Sydney and the United States. I've written books, spoken in more than twenty states, been a guest on hundreds of radio shows, and appeared on national television more times than I can remember. My work has been formally endorsed by former White House press secretaries, movie stars, Senators, presidential candidates, national media, conservative movement icons, and household media personalities. Before that, I was publicly elected to local government office at the age of nineteen and became Australia's youngest ever Deputy Mayor at the age of twenty-one in Sydney.

Because of my high-profile work in America, I can't hold a job in Australia. My first degree was in journalism but because of my political affiliations with the Right, I couldn't find work. In fact, even as a third year student, I was refused an internship at the national broadcaster supposedly because of my elected office, but really because they are biased toward the Left. In the hope of being employable, I trained as a high school teacher, but the last three schools have stopped giving me substitute work, as soon as they've been alerted to Fox News appearances. Yes, that's right. I'm persecuted in Australia by educational and media elites because I go on Fox News. In fact, it has even affected family members as well. The Left in Australia is obsessed with Fox News—for them, no greater evil exists. I have limited ability to earn a living in Australia, and it's because I'm a conservative public figure in America. My country prizes a politics and a culture trademarked with timidity and moderation. By Australian standards, I breach both badly. That's why I'm persona non grata in my own country.

★

I first saw an immigration attorney in September 2009 in Washington DC.

It was an initial consultation that gave me my options. The pleasure cost $700, but the legal gobbledygook and prospect of spending tens of thousands with no guarantee scared me off.

In September 2011, when a lifetime in the US was becoming an increasing reality, my star was rising and my childhood crush had turned into a fully blossomed love affair, I reached out to a Dallas-based immigration law firm about my prospects for an Extraordinary Ability Green Card. In an email, they wrote:

*Based upon the information you provided, this would be an extremely long shot. There is no "bright line" test to determine extraordinary ability . . . . I am adverse to filing petitions that have no chance for success. The absence of a bright line test could favor your petition if we were operating in a culture of "yes." However, the current culture at CIS is one of "no."*

Again, demoralized, I backed away, defeated.

In July 2012, after a major speaking event, a member of the audience sought me out. It emerged in our discussion that she was an immigration attorney. "Really?" I said. "Can you help me?"

"Of course," she said.

This girl could talk. Boy, could this girl talk. And then there was the mutual acquaintance who I trusted that was with her at the event that recommended her. After a couple of phone conversations and some emails, I took the plunge. She was hired. Better yet, she was going to cost much less ($5,000) than I had been quoted before. She seemed friendly, confident, willing to help, and shared my politics. I'd found the right lawyer. *Or so I thought.*

She started work in August. On October 11, I had settled my account with her. All money requested had been paid. Everything she asked of me, I gave her. I was a man on a mission—I wanted to get this done. In November, I grew concerned. Something didn't feel right. She was making excuses, and becoming hostile at questioning. She wouldn't answer her phone, and when I did finally speak to her, she began screaming and accusing me of bullying her "staff." The office she constantly referred to ended up being a meeting room that had to be booked. The receptionist she referenced as hers was just the lady that manned the phones for a dozen different companies in the shared office space. But still I was in denial.

By December, I grew increasingly worried. As I looked over the email and text communications history (which I have kept), it revealed a series of broken promises, contradictory statements, ignored emails, and tardiness. Was she incompetent, lazy, or perhaps just out of her depth? I didn't know. It didn't matter, really. In my opinion, she was manipulative, immature, and deceptive.

As the New Year rolled in, and January 2013 began in earnest, she was still stringing me along. I had no choice.

I told her I'd lost confidence in her.

I threatened her with a complaint to the State Bar of Texas, reminding her that I had all our communications on record, requested a refund, and demanded she send my entire file to an attorney friend of mine in San Diego.

She sent the file, and returned a portion of the money. I wanted to lodge my complaint with the State Bar immediately, but friends and family suggested I wait until my immigration status had been resolved, for fear that her mudslinging could hurt me in the immigration process.

★

Fortunately, that September I had met and become friendly with a wonderful older couple in Austin, Texas, through the Austin Republican Women group. Their son, Doug Jones (currently the national chairman of one of the GOP Presidential candidates), had served in the senior ranks of the Department of Homeland Security under the previous Bush administration. In late January 2013, at the request of his mother, Doug was able to recommend an immigration attorney in New York.

I contacted my attorney friend in San Diego.

It was time to move the file.

★

"The Wolf" was the new attorney, charged with the task of securing my Green Card.

Stern, very serious, and mostly emotionless, he asked me to send him every bit of evidence I had to support the petition, in addition to the file he was about to inherit.

He listened quietly as I travailed him through my previous experience. Refusing to be drawn in, he simply stated he would see what he could use from the work that had been done by the previous attorney.

He also pledged, after reviewing all materials, to tell me whether I had a realistic chance. This was important to me, as I had already expended significant money, been badly burned, and didn't know if this "burning" extended to having been given false hope in the first place.

He explained matter-of-factly that should I proceed, it would cost me between $10,000 to $15,000, and that it would take a very long time. In fact, his exact words were: "It's very expensive, it's very hard, it's very lengthy, there are no guarantees, but it is possible." He said any attorney who offered to do it more cheaply was not telling the truth, or there is something wrong.

★

After sending The Wolf's firm the money he needed in order to look at my case, and inundating him with emails of information as he requested, I sat back and waited.

I contemplated what I would do if the advice was that I couldn't become a permanent resident. Some nights I went to sleep listening to Annie Lennox's soul-stirring song "Why," pondering my predicament. I tried to think positively.

Sure enough, The Wolf came back to me. The news was good. If I did everything he told me to do, we'd have a very good chance. He seemed to be very bureaucratic—not a cage fighter, by any stretch—but that was probably what was needed, I reasoned.

I knew instinctively he was the real deal.

Now, it was time to work.

I set about it with an irrepressible hunger.

Among my tasks: to gather as many letters of recommendation from leaders in my field (the field with which I was claiming extraordinary ability) as possible. I also had to prove my speaking engagements, by securing a letter from the President or Chairman or CEO of every group/organization/conference at which I had ever spoken.

I had begun this with my previous attorney, but contrary to her advice, The Wolf instructed me to get as many as I possibly could.

I did just that. For a period of eight weeks, all day long, all I did was work on getting the necessary documentation ready. I worked day and night, and all this from across the other side of the world.

In the end, I surprised even The Wolf, amassing more than fifty impressive letters from some of the biggest names in America, and hundreds of pages of documented speaking engagements, media appearances, and other assorted evidence. I gave my attorney everything he requested, and more.

★

In early October 2013, on a trip to New York, I met face to face with "The Wolf" (my term of endearment for my attorney) for the first time to, among other things, sign my official application. We even snapped a photograph of the momentous occasion.

On the same trip, I visited with Senators and Congressmen in Washington, DC, in case their assistance would be needed to expedite my application.

On St. Nick's Day in 2013, surely a good omen, finally my application was lodged to the USCIS.

My work was done. We had done our best.

Now, it was all in God's hands.

Three months went by. Then five months. Then eight months. Then Thanksgiving rolled around. Then another St. Nick's Day.

One year, and we'd heard nothing from the USCIS.

Christmas came and went. And then with less than 48 hours left in the year, I received that December 30 email (in fairness, the application had been approved just before Christmas, but my attorney had been away).

Elation. Relief. Joy. We'd gotten there.

U.S. Citizenship and Immigration Services                    I-797, Notice of Action

## THE UNITED STATES OF AMERICA

| RECEIPT NUMBER SRC-14-900-81806 | | CASE TYPE I140 IMMIGRANT PETITION FOR ALIEN WORKER |
|---|---|---|
| RECEIPT DATE December 11, 2013 | PRIORITY DATE December 10, 2013 | PETITIONER ADAMS, NICHOLAS |
| NOTICE DATE December 18, 2014 | PAGE 1 of 1 | BENEFICIARY ADAMS, NICHOLAS |

Notice Type: Approval Notice
Section: Alien of Extraordinary Ability,
Sec.203(b)(1)(A)
Consulate: NVC

The above petition has been approved. We have sent it to the Department of State National Visa Center (NVC), 32 Rochester Avenue, Portsmouth, NH 03801-2909. NVC processes all approved immigrant visa petitions that need consular action. It also determines which consular post is the appropriate consulate to complete visa processing. The NVC will then forward the approved petition to that consulate.

This completes all USCIS action on this petition. You should allow a minimum of 30 days for Department of State processing before contacting the NVC. If you have not received any correspondence from the NVC within 30 days, you may contact the NVC by e-mail at NVCINQUIRY@state.gov. You will need to enter the USCIS receipt number from this approval notice in the subject line. In order to receive information about your petition, you will need to include the Petitioner's name and date of birth, and the Applicant's name and date of birth, in the body of the e-mail.

The NVC will contact the person for whom you are petitioning concerning further immigrant visa processing steps.

The approval of this visa petition does not in itself grant any immigration status and does not guarantee that the alien beneficiary will subsequently be found to be eligible for a visa, for admission to the United States, or for an extension, change, or adjustment of status.

THIS FORM IS NOT A VISA AND MAY NOT BE USED IN PLACE OF A VISA.

The Small Business Regulatory Enforcement and Fairness Act established the Office of the National Ombudsman (ONO) at the Small Business Administration. The ONO assists small businesses with issues related to federal regulations. If you are a small business with a comment or complaint about regulatory enforcement, you may contact the ONO at www.onbudsman.sba.gov or phone 202-205-2417 or fax 202-481-5719.

NOTICE: Although this application/petition has been approved, USCIS and the U.S. Department of Homeland Security reserve the right to verify the information submitted in this application, petition and/or supporting documentation to ensure conformity with applicable laws, rules, regulations, and other authorities. Methods used for verifying information may include, but are not limited to, the review of public information and records, contact by correspondence, the internet, or telephone, and site inspections of businesses and residences. Information obtained during the course of verification will be used to determine whether revocation, rescission, and/or removal proceedings are appropriate. Applicants, petitioners, and representatives of record will be provided an opportunity to address derogatory information before any formal proceeding is initiated.

Please see the additional information on the back. You will be notified separately about any other cases you filed.
IMMIGRATION & NATURALIZATION SERVICE
TEXAS SERVICE CENTER
P O BOX 851488 - DEPT A
MESQUITE   TX   75185-1488
Customer Service Telephone: (800) 375-5283

Form I-797 (Rev. 01/31/05) N

*The original approval of my Extraordinary Ability Green Card Petition.*

Early in the New Year, I had a telephone conversation with my attorney. There were virtual backslaps, and much happiness on both sides of the phone.

"What is next? When can I come?" I asked impatiently.

"Well," The Wolf said, "the heavy lifting is over, but there are still some formalities and some time to go."

The Immigration Service would send the file to the Visa Processing Center in New Hampshire, he explained. Then within thirty days, he would be contacted by the Visa Office, and they would proceed to send him more paperwork—a package of some kind.

The paperwork necessary would include my birth certificate, a national police check, a medical check (to be conducted only by the sole US Consulate-sanctioned medical practice in Sydney), and some other forms.

The final step would be an interview at the US Consulate, which was just a little more than a formality, where they would check my paperwork and ask some basic questions about my approved application.

"About four to five months more to go," The Wolf advised. "Depends on the Consulate—some are slower than others."

★

By March, the final paperwork was submitted.

Now, we had to wait for an interview date at the Consulate.

★

In April 2015, I visited New York.

In what was a reflection of the bond we had formed, The Wolf took me out to lunch at a little Italian restaurant in midtown Manhattan to celebrate our successful petition, and discuss life. The mood was exuberant. I excitedly provided him with recent developments in my own professional career. We had become close, in some ways, a father-son relationship. Things were only looking up.

We just had to wait a little longer.

Two more months went by.

I went about my life, readying myself for my major summer trip—mid-June through mid-July. On June 9, a few days before my flight, the Consulate email I had so long waited for finally arrived.

July 10, the email instructed, I was to present myself at the Sydney Consulate.

"But wait," I thought. "I won't be in Sydney then. I'll still be in New York!"

"No problem," The Wolf said. "We'll reschedule for when you back on July 16. I'll email them."

OK, I thought. End of July, it will be.

The rest of June and all of July went.

While in America, I made my biggest move yet. I decided to set up my own 501(c)(3) Foundation called FLAG.

I was convinced my American Dream had just gone to the next level.

I just knew it was the best idea I'd ever had.

★

On August 1, we had a response.

September 22 was the new interview date. *Another eight weeks?* I groaned inwardly. *Oh, well. At least we had a date.*

In the meantime, to meet the strict medical requirements in preparation for my medical exam, I went to my local doctor to get every vaccine imaginable. Measles, mumps, rubella, flu, diphtheria, tetanus, and pertussis. Fortunately for me, I'd had chicken pox. So, that was one off the list.

In late August, I had my medical exam. It was difficult to get an appointment because as I would discover, the medical center that did conduct the physical exam had a monopoly on the service. If you were immigrating to America, only that Australian doctor could give you the approval you needed.

I was given a full clean bill of health.

★

On September 18, The Wolf and I spoke for thirty minutes.

The purpose of the call? To quickly go over the Consulate interview that would happen in just days.

"Everything will be fine," The Wolf said. "Very routine; there are no trick questions, Nick. Just answer honestly, and have evidence of further work you will conduct once you get to America, and everything will be fine. Be sure to buy your Express Post envelopes, so they can send out your package and immigrant visa, which you will have to present when you physically enter the US on October 8 to formally accept your Green Card."

"Wolf, as I mentioned in my email a couple of weeks ago, they're asking for a copy of my bank account, and I'm loathe to show them—it's very unimpressive," I explained, rather embarrassed.

"Don't worry about it," The Wolf replied The interview will be conducted, corroborating his earlier written response to my email. "They're not really interested in that. They're much more interested in the work you are going to be doing once you get to the United States, so make sure you have your book contract, evidence of speaking engagements etc.

"Anyway," he suggested helpfully, "have it with you, but don't volunteer anything; only provide what you're asked.

"You got this, Nick!"

★

September 22, 2015.

My alarm sounds.

It's 4am. Four hours until my appointment at the Consulate.

The US Consulate in Sydney is in the city center. I live around
90 minutes from there, and I've been warned it might take some
time to get through security.

I walk out of the elevator onto the right floor, clutching my
paperwork, and find eight other people already ahead of me. Four
more arrive soon after I've taken my place in the line. It's only
7:30am.

Security is slow, but quicker than imagined. Turned out the
actual Consulate is on another level, and only a security guard can
send you up the different set of elevators.

★

The Wolf had warned me to expect a process much like a bank or
car registry. You take a number, and wait for it to be called out.
"The interview will be conducted with someone behind a window
and you standing on the other side talking through speakerphone,"
he'd said.

Sure enough, The Wolf had nailed it. Everything looked and felt
just as he had described.

What amazed me was that, with the exception of the sole
American flag in the lobby, and a small, framed photo in one
corner of both President Obama and Vice President Biden, there
was nothing that indicated this was the American Consulate. I
don't quite know what I was expecting, but maybe some coffee
with American creamer, or a couple of photos of one of America's
bigger cities. It didn't feel at all like the American soil it technically
is. It was cold, gray, and ugly.

The first lady to whom I was called up was just in charge of
paperwork. She went through and asked for different documents.
Then as she went through her checklist, she asked, "Oh yes, now
we just need evidence of assets, a bank statement?" As The Wolf
had told me, I gave her a copy of my Australian bank statement.

"OK, Sir," she said. "Just wait, and your number will be called
out again. Someone else will conduct your interview. "

I took my seat.

★

He wore a bowtie.

Couldn't be any older than 45, I thought.

The interview started inauspiciously. Next to this Consular Official was a huge stack of papers—my application.

From his initial very broad questions, two things crossed my mind. Either this was a tactic designed to test the authenticity of the applicant, or he had not read a single word of my application.

I decided on the former.

He tapped some notes into a computer, and then turned to the original paperwork that had been brought in that day. Birth certificate, police certificate, passport, signed passport photographs . . . and bank statement. He pulled it out.

Less than a few minutes in, his line of questioning became focused on my finances. *Do I earn money when I appear on television or radio? How much money did I earn in 2013? How much did I earn in 2014? How many books have I sold? Did I have a job in Australia? How much money had I earned to date in 2015 in Australia?*

I was completely unprepared for these questions, but politely and calmly answered them best I could. *Why are you asking me these questions,* I asked myself. *I have the best attorney in the business, painfully meticulous, and I told him twice I was worried about showing my bank statement as it was "unimpressive," and both times he said it wasn't a problem. This Consulate guy has no clue what he is talking about,* my mind raged.

As if reading my mind, he asked me to "please just wait here." For ten agonizing minutes, he disappeared. When he returned, he said words to the effect of: "Mr. Adams, we can't process your visa today, as you have failed to provide evidence of sufficient assets. If you look at this table here, you are required to earn either a $19,912 annual salary, or prove you have over $60,000 in assets. That's US dollars," he hastily added.

"So, what happens now?" I asked. "It's taken me a long time to get here. I'm meant to immigrate on October 8!" He nodded, emotionless. "Well," he said, as he filled out a yellow sheet of paper, underlining an email address and checking the "Evidence of Support" box. "You need to send in further evidence either by email or post, and if that is to my satisfaction, we will send out your visa and paperwork. Otherwise I will just send back your passport. I can't guarantee it'll be done by the 8th. We always advise people never to make travel arrangements, as immigration is an unpredictable business."

*So, that's it??* I wanted to scream. *You've got the gall to ask me about money. Do you know how much it has cost me just to have the pleasure of standing in front of you? $30,000, and all for nothing? Do you realize I have no assets because I have poured everything into my dreams, every last cent? And anyway, isn't the American dream all about coming with nothing and making everything?*

Instead, I bit my lip. "Can I go home now?"

"Yes," he said. "We're finished for today."

"Thank you," I squeaked.

I hadn't even had a chance to offer him the evidence of the work that I would continue with in America that I had brought along.

★

As soon as I was reacquainted with my cell phone, stored with security, I frantically tried to reach The Wolf. No luck. I sent emails. No response. More calls. Only voicemail. *There had to be an explanation,* I thought. How could he not have told me? In fact, I had raised it with him specifically, twice! I even had it in writing. He was right about everything else—*how could he have got it so wrong?*

I could have easily had money transferred into my bank account; easily had assets transferred into my name. This could have been avoided!

★

Less than an hour after leaving the Consulate, I had the sum of $200,000 deposited into my account, courtesy of my father.

Finally, that night (morning in New York), The Wolf called.

I explained what had happened. He listened carefully. As I told him about the financial requirements the Consular official had revealed, he said quietly, almost muttering to himself, "That's not true. Not true."

"So, he's wrong?" I asked eagerly.

"Yes, he is Nick, but that isn't the question to ask. It doesn't matter that he's wrong. In a sense, he's right. He's the one that makes the final decision, and if that's what he thinks, then we have no choice but to give him what he wants.

"Send me the evidence of all your future work, as well as the new bank statement, and a formal legal document from your father explaining this is a gift," The Wolf demanded.

I said I would.

With the conversation drawing to a close, I had to ask the burning question.

"Why didn't you tell me, Wolf? This could have been so easily avoided…"

Firmly, unapologetically and without hesitation, The Wolf said, "Because I didn't think it was necessary, Nick."

And that was that.

★

Four days later, we had submitted our evidence, and delicately asked if possible, for the paperwork to be sent in time, so that I could still proceed with my planned October 8 flight.

It was September 26.

Once more, we were playing the waiting game.

★

On September 27, my father fell violently ill. The next few days were brutal.

In between fevers and shivering, he was coughing blood, struggling to breathe, his stomach was bloated to ridiculous proportion, and he was aching all over. Not to mention, he had this incredibly dry mouth that would just not go away.

*Pneumonia.*

My father had pneumonia.

★

He was sicker than I had ever seen. In a move absolutely shocking to anyone that knew him, he was even prepared to admit himself to the hospital.

★

By Tuesday, October 6, the disease had been vanquished by strong antibiotics, but had now been replaced with a relentless weakness.

He was barely able to move.

★

Every day I walked to the letterbox looking for notice of a parcel, and every day I walked back empty-handed and heavy-hearted.

October 8 came and went. My flight left, without me.

The Wolf sent me an encouraging email:

*Hi Nick: I contacted the Consulate again on Tuesday, and am awaiting their reply. If I do not hear anything in the next few days I will call them. Stay strong!*
*Regards. The Wolf*

The only thing I could think about was, *Maybe it's a good thing I'm stuck here, so I can help my mom with my dad.*

**E-Ticket Itinerary & Receipt**

Your Booking Reference

**Z2RFET**

**Important Information**

- This is your E-Ticket Itinerary & Receipt. You must bring it with you to the airport for check-in, and it is recommended you retain a copy for your records.
- Each passenger travelling needs a printed copy of this document for immigration, customs, airport security checks and duty free purchases.
- Please familiarise yourself with the key Conditions of Carriage, Dangerous Goods guide and other information attached.
- For travel to the USA under the Visa Waiver Program you must obtain an electronic authorisation through the Electronic System for Travel Authorisation website before you board your flight.

**Passenger Ticket Information**

| Passenger Name | Frequent Flyer No. | Ticket No. | Issued | Ticket Total* |
|---|---|---|---|---|
| Mr Nicholas Adams | | 081-2461314288 | 25 Aug 15 | 1,629.38 |
| | Frequent Flyer Silver / oneworld Ruby | | | |
| | | Ticket Total for all passengers* | | 1,629.38 |

*Amounts are displayed in Australian Dollars (AUD)

**Your Itinerary**

| Date | Flight Number | Departing | Arriving | Status | Flight Information |
|---|---|---|---|---|---|
| 08 Oct 15 | QF7 | Sydney 1400, 2:00PM Terminal 1 | Dallas/Fort Worth Intl 1305, 1:35PM 08 Oct 15 Terminal D | Economy Confirmed | Est journey Time: 16:35 Non-Stop Aircraft Type: Airbus Industrie A380 |
| 14 Dec 15 | QF8 | Dallas/Fort Worth Intl 2010, 8:10PM Terminal D | Sydney 0605, 6:05AM 16 Dec 15 Terminal 1 | Economy Confirmed | Est journey Time: 16:55 Non-Stop Aircraft Type: Airbus Industrie A380 |

**Payment Details**

| Date | Payment Type | Reference | Amount* |
|---|---|---|---|
| 25 Aug 15 | American Express | | 1,629.38 |

This may appear as multiple transactions on your credit card statement

**Your Receipt Details**

| Ticket Charges | Charges | GST | Total* |
|---|---|---|---|
| Total* | 1,629.38 | | |
| Card Payment Fee | 00.00 | | |
| Total Amount Payable* | 1,629.38 | 0.00 | 1,629.38 |

*Includes Taxes/Fees/carrier Charges

**Tax Information**

GST does not apply to international travel. No tax invoice will be issued.

Issued by
**Qantas Airways**

**Flying With Us**

**Before Check-in**
- Ensure that each passenger carries a printed copy of this document when traveling.
- Have necessary visas and the minimum passport validity required for the countries you are visiting.
- Label your bags inside and out with your name, address and contact number at your destination.
- Check Carry-on baggage and checked baggage allowances as restrictions apply.

**Getting Away On Time**
- Ensure you are at the airport with enough time to complete necessary check-in, security screening and, for international flights, customs and immigration.
- Familiarise yourself with the check-in and boarding times. Information for Qantas and QantasLink flights is in the Travel Information section attached.

**Check-in**
- Visit qantas.com/checkin to choose the check-in option best for you.

Qantas Airways Limited ABN 16 009 661 901. 10 Bourke Road, Mascot NSW 2020, Australia
qantas.com

*The flight with which I was meant to immigrate. October 8, 2015 Flight Itinerary from Qantas.*

★

October 9 began well enough.

A spirited morning session at the gym, and a father on the mend, albeit slowly. With the October 8 albatross off my neck, I was ready to wait it out.

I showered, and emerged feeling fresh. I noticed I had missed a call. I listened to the voicemail. It was a young lady's voice:

*"Hi. This is a message for Nicholas. I'm calling from the US Consulate in Sydney in regards to your Immigrant Visa Application. Just ringing in regard to your passport and returning it to you, because we have yet to issue the visa. A follow-up email will be sent to you now to advise. Alright. Thank you."*

No sooner had I finished transcribing the voicemail and emailing it to The Wolf, then I received a separate email from him. It was an email I had been copied on. It was a response to the Consulate. Immediately, I sensed the disbelief and anger in The Wolf. He was measured, but only just. For a man known for his calmness, his email reeked emotion.

Turns out at almost the same time I was listening to my Voicemail, The Wolf had received the email the young lady had said she would send. It read:

*At this time, we cannot issue the visa for Mr. Adams. We tried to contact Mr. Adams on his mobile today, unfortunately with no such luck. Mr. Adams can collect his passport from our office today October 9, 2015 at 2:30pm or alternatively, please provide a suitable mailing address in Australia and we can send the passport to Mr. Adams via express post.*

The Wolf's fiery email where he referred to the above email as "startling," and reminded them that "this comes after a very long and exhaustive visa petition process, which included a thorough review of Mr. Adams' achievements and credentials, and which resulted in the approval of his status as an individual of extraordinary ability by the USCIS," appeared to have the desired effect.

The Consulate soon appeared to walk back their apparent rejection, writing back:

*The application is under further review by the consular officer at this time.*

★

I spoke to The Wolf that night.

He explained he was stunned. Hadn't seen anything like it in 35 years of experience. The correspondence was strange. The questions at the interview were strange. The way they had given no reasons was strange.

He was heartened, though, by their revision to the original email, where they said it was under further review. He said he just couldn't see how they could possibly deny the application.

We agreed I would not collect my passport, or ask for it to be sent back, as it was better to leave it with them so the process could always still be quickly completed.

There was an appeal process to the State Department, but it was long and arduous, The Wolf informed me. It was unsaid, but I also knew he wanted to say "expensive."

The Wolf said we might need to call on my political and media contacts to win the court of public opinion, if all else failed. I sighed.

"Tell me, Wolf, while this sorts itself out, if I do get my passport, can I still come to America on my Visa Waiver [the 90 day pass all tourists/visitors to the US get]?"

The Wolf cleared his throat.

With regret rich in his voice, "Well, Nick, there is a hard and fast rule that's been around for decades that anyone who has shown 'immigrant intent' by applying for permanent residency, can never be allowed to return to the United States."

My heart stopped and my mind raced. "What do you mean?" I asked. "I can never ever travel to the US again, if my application is rejected?"

The Wolf avoided the question. "We're not there yet; we can talk about that later. There hasn't been a rejection. Let's just focus on doing what we can to get this through."

★

Meanwhile, my legal fees continue to stack up. This can't go on forever.

★

Today is four weeks to the day since my Consulate interview.

I haven't shaved since that day. I won't either, until things have resolved. In a small but significant way, it's a welcome change for me, and one that reflects my minimalist approach right now.

I continue to work toward my American dream, as though it will all be resolved. For six and a half years, all I've lived and breathed is America. Right now, I am preparing the marketing of my new book out in February with my publishers. I keep my sanity by spending hours at the gym, eating right, changing my routine, going for long walks, doing household chores, spending time with my parents, listening to motivational speakers, and taking many showers that alternate between hot and cold.

I've stopped social media, and largely withdrawn from social activity. I'm more than anxious that I may never again be able to travel to the US. It has dawned on me that I may never be able to take a future wife to Hawaii for a vacation. That I might have to tell the child tugging at my sleeve in the future, begging to go once to Disneyland like all his friends at school, that I can't go with him.

And why? I've done *nothing* wrong. I've been to America sixteen times. I've never overstayed. I've never broken the law. *In fact, all I've done, is follow the law.*

My family and I don't want to appeal. It's not only the money. All an appeal will do is sully my reputation, and make America harder for me. I'll forever be open to the attack: *This is the guy that the nation once said we don't want?* No, thank you.

I pray every night.

My father remains weak, but thank God, gets stronger with each passing day. The only upshot of this nightmare has been my ability to spend more time with him.

★

6 November, 2015.

It's been more than six weeks now since my Consulate interview. Four weeks since the bizarre phone message instructing me to pick up my passport.

The same attorney friend who helped me between the disastrous Texan experience and the New York one decided to reach out to two other specialist immigration attorneys in San Diego with great reputations in that part of the world. Both have since corroborated The Wolf: according to them, the minimum assets/bank/finance stuff the Consulate raised is total "bull… That's three attorneys now singing the same tune.

And anyway, with two employment offers, and the money in my account, the "bull" doesn't even matter anymore . . . they couldn't even rely on it if they wanted to.

But I wonder: *Did this guy really just make it up? Was it just an excuse? Would they have found something else, if the $200,000 had already been in the account? Maybe they were just looking for excuses?*

The two San Diegans also said that they (the US Consulate in Sydney) are *"certainly disguising"* the real reason it's taking so long.

Incompetence? Federal government inefficiency? Or deliberate sabotage? Is it my *politics*? Everyone seems to want to choose the latter.

I enlist the help of the Office of U.S. Senator Cory Gardner. "They have my passport," I say. "They've had it for six weeks!!" The Senator's Office made a formal inquiry, but even they haven't heard back yet.

My dad is much better, but this is tearing our family apart emotionally. The delay, the uncertainty, the helplessness— it's killing all of us. It's torture. Six weeks now, I have been in complete limbo. My life is, effectively, on hold, and it is the worst feeling in the world. The situation needs to be resolved quickly and smoothly, because I (we) can't live like this.

What is happening now with the immigration process is potentially career-breaking, dream-shattering, and life-changing.

In order to be eligible to be an American citizen, you need to have been a Green Card holder for five years.

There is nothing more I want to be than an American. *But does America want me?*

I have a very limited future in Australia. *Possibly none.*

*But if America is off the cards, what do I do?* It's too unbearable even to contemplate.

Do I turn back, or do I press on?

I've fought, scratched and clawed to have a chance at the greatest privilege of them all—being an American.

I've done it the *right* way.

So, can someone please explain why everything feels so *wrong*?

Right now, I'm homeless. In a world full of so-called refugees flooding countries, I'm one that will never be discussed.

*Please, God, intervene.* Please stop the torture.

★

Friday, the 13 of November.

My worst nightmare materializes.

The postman delivers a flimsy plastic 3kg Express Post envelope. I recognize it as one of the ones I had to provide to the US Consulate at my interview.

But it doesn't contain much. Just my Australian passport, and one sheet of paper.

The sheet of paper is a three-paragraph letter from the Consulate in Sydney.

It informs me that administrative processing of my immigrant visa case has been completed, and that my file had been returned to the USIC Service Center in the US, where it had been filed with a recommendation from the Consulate that the approval be revoked. It says that the United States Citizenship and Immigration Service (USCIS) will make a final determination.

It is simply signed Vice Consul, with an indecipherable scribble as the signature.

**CONSULATE GENERAL OF THE UNITED STATES**
LEVEL 59   MLC CENTRE   19-29 MARTIN PLACE   SYDNEY NSW 2000
61-2-9373-9200   http://sydney.usconsulate.gov/sydney

November 10, 2015

Mr. Nicholas Adams

Dear Mr. Adams,

This letter is in reference to your U.S. immigrant visa petition, USCIS receipt number SRC1490081806.

We have concluded administrative processing of this immigrant visa case. After a review of the petition, the interview testimony and documents submitted, we have returned it to the USIC Service Center on November 10, 2015, where it will be filed with a recommendation for revocation. A final determination on your case will be made after USCIS has finished its review.

From this point forward, you should contact USCIS with any additional questions regarding the status of your case. Please note that it will be several weeks before USCIS receives your file from Sydney, as it will be sent through official mail.

Yours respectfully,

Vice Consul
United States Consulate General Sydney

Enclosure:  Passport

*Too gutless to give his name. The letter from the US Consulate confirming my worst nightmare.*

★

So, there you have it.

No name. No reasons. Nothing.

Just: "recommended for revocation." In other words, the Consulate is asking the USCIS to revoke my approved Green Card petition.

★

Seven weeks has been seven rounds.

Rounds in a prize fight that has never been a competitive contest, since that initial flurry of blows wreaked havoc on my self-belief, confidence, and optimism. I've gone from champion to contender. From vanquisher to survivor, from winner to loser.

I'm out on my feet. Against the ropes. I'm absorbing incredible punishment. My body prays for the mercy of the knockout. My mind refuses to comply. Only blind, brave instinct has so far managed to evade my opponent's biggest haymakers. As my opponent circles, looking to land the final knockout blow to the chin, I can barely make him out through my two swollen eyes. Vainly, I put my hands up one last time.

Then it came.

The knockout punch.

My favorite motivational speaker, Les Brown, always says: "If life knocks you down, try and land on your back. Because if you can look up, you can get up. And if you get up, you can stand up. And if you stand up, you can fight for your dream once again."

But I couldn't even manage that this time.

When I hit the ground, I was face down.

★

I scan the letter, and send it to The Wolf.

Both my parents have lost color. All our money—and for what? And why? And how could we be treated so poorly?

Why would a representative of the country I love so much be so awful to me?

The Wolf's response was quick, and sharp.

*Hi Nick:*

*This is extremely disturbing and disheartening, to say the least. Consuls have the ability to challenge decisions made by the Immigration Service (approving immigrant visa petitions or applications) when they feel that an application/ petition was approved in error. In other words, the consul can challenge a decision made by the Immigration Service if s/he believes that it was made in error.*

*The authority to do this is used sparingly, and I am stunned that this was done in your case; especially after the volume of evidence and documentation presented to the Immigration Service, and the fact that your petition was approved without question. It is apparent that the consul has concluded that your petition was approved in error, and that you are/were not qualified to classification as an individual of extraordinary ability.*

*What is particularly egregious is that the consul did not give you/us the opportunity to respond to the underlying basis of your eligibility, and only focused on the financial question—which we addressed. Equally as distressing is that the consul did not question your credentials at the time of the interview. I find the consul's actions to be a gross abuse of discretion and authority. I think that there is more to this than appears on the surface, but what it is I cannot determine.*

*The Immigration Service will now reconsider its decision, and I am certain that the consul has presented your case in a most unfavorable light in order to influence the Immigration Service to revoke the approval of the petition.*

*We can discuss the strategy going forward, and whether we can marshal enough political support to intervene, but I fear that we are now facing a lengthy and difficult review process.*

*I will call you tomorrow with next steps.*

★

11pm here. That night I talk with The Wolf on the phone.

Defeat is rich in his voice too. His frustration is abundant; he sounds very much like a man used to getting his way.

But he insists I must continue on. "You have to fight this," he says. "It'll be a very long fight, but I know you will win ultimately." But he offers little in the way of action he is going to take. He says we could take it to the Federal Court—"I am sure a judge there would be equally as appalled as me at this and grant in your favor"— but it would be ridiculously expensive, somewhere in the vicinity of $150,000. Otherwise, we just have to wait for the decision of USCIS, and then keep fighting. I ask if we'll get a hearing with USCIS before they make the decision about whether to agree or disagree with the Consulate. He says no. I ask him again to please explain the issue surrounding entry to the United States. He tells me what he has previously told me—he's not certain because this is pretty unchartered territory, but as an intending immigrant, he doesn't think I can visit until all this has been sorted. Before he goes, I reiterate there are very limited resources left with which to fight this. He brushes this off, and then proposes I set up a "Legal Fundraising for Nick Adams Committee." "Wolf," I say, incredulous, how on earth do you propose I do that, when I can't even be in the country?"

I lay down to sleep, and can't remember a time I felt so helpless. Everything I had worked for. Everything I had worked toward. All lost? How could this be? Tears creep into my eyes, and gently roll down my cheeks, spilling onto my doona, as I desperately try to sleep.

★

I'm woken by the kookaburras laughing outside my room.

It takes just a split second for the recollections of yesterday's events to flood my mind. I groan, and sink back into bed. I reach for the covers and fling them to the side violently, almost as though anything less wouldn't suffice in getting me up.

I splash cold water on my face, and apprehensively walk to where my Blackberry had spent the night charging.

Sitting in my email inbox are multiple emails from The Wolf. He has reached out to Doug Jones (who originally referred me to The Wolf), who just happens to be in the middle of running a Presidential campaign, and others, informing them of what has happened, and asking for their time on the phone to discuss a strategy.

But one email is a letter from The Wolf to me.

It's about the existing balance on my account. There are also legal fees for the setup of FLAG that have mounted. *Nick, I know it's a difficult time for you and your family, but . . . .*

The law firm wants its money quicker. "Use a portion of the money your dad gave you for the Consulate," The Wolf urges, rather forwardly. "This is not over, and I believe that you will prevail in the end," he insists.

I feel a headache start to build.

It's enough to send me straight back to bed.

★

Desperate to relieve my mind of my awful predicament, I reach for the remote control. I glance at the clock on the wall. *Well, that's good,* I tell myself, *I can spoil myself and at least watch my favorite show—The Five* [it's on Tuesday–Saturday mornings, Australian time].

But it's Shephard Smith—reporting live on the attacks underway in Paris. Shep is the best in the business, and it shows.

What is the world coming to?

★

The Wolf's letter has upset me.

There are some things that need to be said. *Neither of us could have seen this coming, but he's got to understand that the legal funds to fight this are exhausted.* This is not just simply a matter of we're going to pay whatever it costs to get the outcome we want, and bankrupt ourselves in the process.

It occurs to me that most of his clients, and those of this New York firm, are unlikely to be individuals like me. They're most likely major businesses with near unlimited funds that engage him to sort immigration matters for their employees, and bear whatever cost that entails. This is why cost never seems to factor into any of his advice, despite my frequently voiced concerns.

I make a substantial payment toward the balance, and then I start writing a very difficult letter, that would undergo at least a dozen drafts.

★

I make it clear that I will pay him every cent the firm has charged me, but that it will take time.

I explain that I based my decision to form a charitable foundation on his immigration advice, where he had told me and we had celebrated that the "heavy lifting had been done" and that the last step in this matter was the US Consulate interview in Sydney, which would be little more than a formality. And I also tell him that I know that his assistance connecting me with his colleagues to set up the 501(c)(3) was based on his belief that the visa would be granted too.

Since April, when just the Consulate interview was remaining, my immigration matter has cost an additional $8,000. *Please be aware that this balance was totally unexpected, as were the unforeseen circumstances*, I write. *However, the end result is that funds for the immigration matter have been completely exhausted. There is no more money. I have expressed this in the past, and it still remains the case.*

I continue:

*I like to honor my obligations, and that is why the financial consideration is a major concern for me. It is also why I need to tell you to stop acting on my behalf if it results in more being charged to my account. I want to come to America to live and work, and I know you would like to see my immigrant visa granted, but as things stand now, it seems unlikely without further legal costs—costs that I cannot incur and cannot afford for the time being. However, when that time does come, I'll provide my explicit authorization to you in writing. Until then, please do not undertake any more actions that will result in additional legal fees, government fees, or any other fees related to my immigration case being charged to my account, save for minimal expenses that may be necessary to incur for the forwarding of documents and updates received by you of which I should be made aware.*

I finish with this plea: *please consider continuing any legal work on a pro bono basis.*

★

As the days languish on, my frustration grows. The Consulate's unexplained, unexpected, and highly unusual actions over the past weeks have been torturous. What was meant to be procedural turned out to be disastrous. *How could this happen*, I asked myself dozens of times a day.

I can't get The Wolf's words out of my mind: "I think there is more to this than appears on the surface, but what it is I cannot determine."

In all the emails and letters from the Consulate, there is not a single name. Standard practice for American Consulates and Embassies worldwide. The penultimate letter was simply signed "Vice Consul." But on the day of the interview, although his name tag had been obscured, I had caught the first six letters of the interviewer's name. Was it the same guy? I doubt it, but you never know.

*There must be a way,* I thought, *of tracking this Vice Consul down.* If anyone can do it, it's me.

★

I began my electronic search, assiduously chasing every lead. My eyes began to swim and my back began to ache, from combing through page after page of Google search results.

But I was on a mission.

★

I find an official Australian government document from the Department of Foreign Affairs and Trade, dealing in protocol for foreign diplomats, which lists every foreign dignitary, where they serve, the capacity in which they serve, and their partner's name.

Listed under the US Consulate in Sydney are several Vice Consuls. I scan their names, and one leaps out immediately. The six letters match—*could I have finally found the source of my misery*, I wonder.

According to this document, this Vice Consul's partner is a man.

But I need visual proof. I've seen this guy's face.

*He interviewed me*, I tell myself.

*I can ID him.*

★

I scramble to open Facebook.

I type in the name. I click on it. I see his profile picture.

FOUND HIM!!! GOT HIM!!! That's the guy who interviewed me!!! He's a Vice Consul!

I found the bastard.

★

Immediately, it becomes obvious to me.

This official's sexual and political orientation is the opposite of mine.

His Facebook page reveals support of gay activism, and Democratic politicians.

I hit all the social networks, searching for him, gathering whatever I can find, without alerting him that I'm on to him.

As I go and swim laps at the local pool that night, I swim with the intensity of an Olympian, mind swirling, heart racing, body trembling but finally with loose shoulders.

In my mind, I knew exactly what had happened, although I couldn't prove a thing.

For tonight, just that knowledge was enough.

★

It is abundantly clear to me what has happened.

Anyone with my life experience would.

It all made sense.

Come pick your passport up on the 9th . . . one day <u>after</u> you knew I was meant to fly to America, because I'd told you. *The arrogance*.

The lack of explanation or provided reasons.

The seven-and-a-half weeks delay in providing a response, and returning my passport.

This man thought he knew me from the documents that had been lodged, and didn't like me because of my politics. I suspect he took offence to things I have said in the US media concerning support for the traditional family and gender roles. *Had he found out about FLAG*, I wondered? About its plans to lead a conservative, patriotic renaissance, and expose the Left?

I believe this man acted arrogantly and abused his position because he wanted to vilify an enemy of the Left.

So many people in America had told me over the years that they feared the Left was ensuring changing demographics to secure a permanent role in political leadership in the long-term. They only want people who are going to vote Democrat, they would tell me. Turns out they were right. The strategy even extends to legal immigration.

But how on earth could I prove it?

And most important, how could I salvage my application?

★

Days pass. Then weeks. It's now early December.

A decision must be made. My upcoming, new book *Retaking America: Crushing Political Correctness* is due to be released February 23.

I need to be in America for the book tour. But can I fly to America? Should I fly to America? Will they let me in? If you are turned away at a port of entry in the United States, it is an automatic five-year ban. The Wolf has put the fear of God in me. *But I haven't done anything wrong, dammit*, I think to myself, with clenched teeth.

I ask my father for his advice. His instruction? "Go. F'em. You haven't done anything wrong. You're going to have a return ticket to Australia, which you can show them. You don't have any immigrant intent. Show them your book when you enter. You're not breaking any laws. You've worked so hard to get here—just go. It won't be a problem, trust me. Otherwise you're just going to be doing what you've done the last couple of months—sitting around here, paralyzed, moping around, upset, and not looking forward to anything. You need to get back on track.

I realize how hard it must be for him and my mother to have watched the impact this has had on their son. My famed confidence has really taken a hit.

*Screw 'em,* I echoed. I've got to live my life. I'm in the right. I remembered the motto of Texas Ranger Bill McDonald: *"No man in the wrong can stand up against a fellow that's in the right and keeps on a-comin'."*

I book the flight. January 25 is the day I will fly to America.

★

It's December 11.

Today I go to the hospital for corrective jaw surgery, an operation thirty-one years in the making, a hangover from the chemotherapy and radiation I had as a child to beat cancer.

Two broken jaws equal six weeks of a liquid/soft food diet, little exercise and major bed rest. Talking, my favorite pastime, isn't too easy, either! *God, take me now.*

Oh well. It was always going to have to get done.

May as well do it now.

★

The days of recovery go slowly by, but I am buoyed by the upcoming trip to America.

Meanwhile, in great news, pre-orders of my new book— *Retaking America: Crushing Political Correctness*—are really taking off.

Christmas and New Year's Eve come and go.

With little else to do, I plug away at plans for America on my iPad during bed-rest.

★

Friday, January 22.

The braces and bands come out, and my surgeon gives me the all-clear to travel to America on Monday. Most important, I can eat steak again!

We're on.

★

Monday, January 25.

*Wheels down.* Its 1:35pm as the Qantas A380 leisurely makes its way across the tarmac and toward the gate, after a successful landing at the Dallas-Fort Worth Airport.

It's been a long fifteen-and-half hour flight, direct from Sydney. As the superjumbo jet had turned over Lake Grapevine for its final descent, and as we got lower to the ground, I caught a glimpse of an interstate and spotted several pick-up trucks. My heart grinned. I must have looked pretty goofy to any fellow passengers, who had the misfortune of happening to see me.

★

My feelings are mixed.

I'm happy to be off the plane. Excited to finally be back in the country I love.

But now what?

Will my entry go smoothly? I clutch my book, and return ticket closely.

I begin the long walk to the customs hall.

★

As I take my spot in the Non-US Passport Holder/Non-Green Card Holder line, I look over rather wistfully at the Green Card Holder Line.

I take a deep breath.

Soon, there is just one person in front of me. Then, it's just me, waiting to be waved over, ready to respond to the call of "*Next!*"

My heart is beating fast. My palms are sweaty. Butterflies swim in my stomach. *This is so wrong*, I think to myself. *I feel like a criminal about to commit a crime. And I'm anything but.* For the six thousandth time, I vow revenge on the man that is putting me through this.

"*NEXT!*" comes the shout.

★

"G'day, Sir," I stammer, as I hand over my passport and my blue Customs Declaration Form.

"Hello," the young Hispanic officer says. "What's the purpose of your visit today?"

"I'm actually here on a book tour, Sir. I have a brand new book coming out, actually here it is," I rambled, without stopping to take a breath, flashing the book around like it was a weapon. Luckily for me, on the book's front cover was a photo of me.

"Oh, wow, that's interesting," he says, picking the book up.

I smile. "It's my dream to hit the New York Times bestseller list," I explain.

"That's great," he says, "you always gotta chase your dreams.

"How long will your visit be? Do you have a return ticket?"

He scans my passport, and invites me to do the obligatory hand and thumb prints, followed by the headshot photograph.

"OK, Mr. Adams," he says, closing my passport and handing it back. "You're good to go." I thank him and begin walking away.

"Hey," he calls out. "Give me a look at that book again. I may just grab myself a copy. Want you to get that dream."

For the first time in months, I relax. God, I love this country.

★

My trip is a stunning success.

Before March 1, I travel from Dallas to St Louis to New York to New Hampshire to Oregon and back to New Hampshire. From there, I travel to Charleston and then to Dallas, and then back to Charleston. Then New York again, followed by DC. Speaking events, media appearances—*Retaking America: Crushing Political Correctness* takes off, and becomes a best-seller.

Amidst it all, I take the opportunity to gather as much political support from as many Congressional and Senatorial offices as possible.

By mid-February, I have half a dozen Senators and more than a dozen Congressmen who are formally expressing an interest in my case, directly to the United States Citizenship and Immigration Service.

★

As I finish a radio interview conducted by phone in my midtown-Manhattan hotel room, I look outside. 6pm. It's dark. It's been a long but productive day. Dinner is not for another ninety minutes. Enough time for a bit of a laydown.

On my bedside table, my Blackberry blinks.

I pick it up. It's an email from Senator Cory Gardner's office.

It reads:

*Hello, Mr. Adams!*

*I just received an e-mail from the Texas Service Center advising U.S. Citizenship and Immigration Services (USCIS) reviewed your Form I-140, and it was approved/reaffirmed on January 13, 2016, and shipped to the National Visa Center (NVC) for Consular processing.*

*I will contact the National Visa Center to see what the status of your case is with their office, then I will report back to you.*

*Please let me know if you have any questions.*

Can it . . . ? No way!!!! For real?? That's great news!!!

I sit there rather dumbstruck.

I read the email over and over and over again.

But something is bothering me.

Something is not right.

Then it dawns on me. The date didn't make sense. January 13. How could my petition have been re-approved/re-affirmed on January 13? It was too early for a decision to have been made, firstly, and secondly, why would I have been finding out almost six weeks later?

More than that, with almost twenty different offices on the Hill working my case, why was I only hearing this from one of them?

I send several emails back to Senator Gardner's office. I say, "Look, I want to believe this, and it's not that I don't trust you, but are you sure? The dates just don't match up. Can I see it for my own eyes?"

Soon, I get a PDF of the email that Senator Gardner's office received from USCIS. The name and contact information has all been redacted, but the email is clear.

I'm still not convinced.

**From:**          Texas Service Center Congressional Unit
**Sent:**          Wednesday, February 24, 2016 1:54 PM
**To:**
**Subject:**      RE: 114-100335 Adams CRM:0673309

Greetings:

Thank you for your inquiry on behalf of your constituent, Mr. Nicholas Adams, regarding his pending Form I-140 Immigrant Petition for Alien Worker.

To address your constituent's concerns, U.S. Citizenship and Immigration Services (USCIS) reviewed that the Form I-140 was approved/reaffirmed on 1/13/2016 and shipped to the National Visa Center (NVC) for Consular processing. For further assistance please contact NVC directly at:

We hope this information is helpful. If we may be of further assistance, please let us know.

Sincerely,

Immigration Services Officer

Congressional Unit

USCIS - Texas Service Center

*The email that had been sent in error, suggesting my petition had been re-affirmed.*

I delay any celebrations, and send an email to the lady I know best. *Patricia Sykes.* She works for Senator Graham.

I ask her to confirm it for me.

I sleep surprisingly well that night, but I am on tenterhooks from the moment I get up.

The next morning at around 11am, I get a call. It's Sykes.

She confirms my suspicion.

A senior officer at USCIS had made an error. The email was sent in error. An email correcting the record and apologizing for the error had just been sent out to all the Offices involved in my case.

No decision had yet been made on my petition, Sykes said. It was still being assessed.

"How incompetent are these people?" my father muttered angrily, as I relayed the news to him and my mother. "How can they play with us like that? How can you make a mistake like that?"

Yet another unbelievable turn.

★

I visit The Wolf in his office, for an hour.

We speak about things.

As I update him on my lobbying efforts, and then press him on the specifics of what will next transpire, he gives it to me straight. This is unchartered territory for him. He tells me in his thirty-five years of practicing immigration law he has never seen a 'consular return.' He has never had a client with an approved petition who has gone to interview at the Consulate or Embassy in their home country, and then had their application returned with an adverse recommendation to the US Immigration Service. This has never happened to him before.

I leave feeling much better. The Wolf is a good man, and an outstanding attorney. It's just a ridiculous set of circumstances that have presented themselves. These immigration laws are so dense and indecipherable that regularly I have been getting inconsistent answers from attorneys who practice in this area. And then you throw in on top of that someone who decides to give you a hard time, and you get chaos.

As I walk the thirty minutes back to my hotel in the New York chill, I reflect on the absurdity of life sometimes.

You can do all the right things, have all the right connections, have the best attorney, pay all the money you have, and sometimes you still get screwed.

★

Super Tuesday in America.

One of my life goals is achieved as I do live election analysis on the Fox Business Network that night.

The next morning, on March 2, I travel by Amtrak from New York's Penn Station to Washington DC's Union Station.

I was here for CPAC—the Conservative Political Action Conference—held at The Gaylord Convention Center, in National Harbor, Maryland.

That afternoon as I sit in an Advisory Council meeting of Turning Point USA, my Blackberry again blinks.

This time it is Congressman Joe Barton's office.

*Nick, please see below.~ Jodi*

*Thank you for your inquiry on behalf of your constituent, Nicholas Adams, regarding his I-140 Petition (SRC1490081806).*

*USCIS records show that this petition was re-affirmed approved on today, March 02, 2016. It will be sent back to the NVC.*

*Please let us know if we can be of any further assistance.*

Instinctively, my hand formed a fist.

WOW! And this time the date makes sense!

But I cautioned myself. Once bitten, twice shy. Or in my case, thrice bitten, quadruple shy.

*We will wait until we hear it from others,* I told myself sternly.

Immediately, I reach out to my other contacts and ask for confirmation.

★

Amid the chaos of Radio Row at CPAC on March 3, I get confirmation of the incredible from Patricia Sykes by phone. Only moments earlier I had prayed with my friend, fellow Texan, and nationally syndicated radio host, Pastor Greg Young, about receiving good news.

USCIS has thrown out the recommendation for revocation of the original approval, and re-affirmed their original decision. My Green Card petition has been approved, for the second time!!!

The emails come in thick and fast. I field calls from multiple Senatorial and Congressional Offices, all bearing the great news.

I feel elation.

I feel relief.

I feel victory.

I feel vindication.

I feel justice.

I know we are not completely out of the woods yet. The petition will now be returned to the National Visa Center, and then back to the Consulate in Sydney to get the immigrant visa. It's an indispensable part of the process.

But it's the best news ever. Now, I just have to wait for another interview date from the Consulate.

*Surely,* I say to myself, *they're not going to try and pull the same rubbish again.* This time I could even walk in naked, and they'd have to give it to me!

I vow to expose it all, when all is done and dusted.

Department of Homeland Security
U.S. Citizenship and Immigration Services                    **Form I-797C, Notice of Action**

---

**THIS NOTICE DOES NOT GRANT ANY IMMIGRATION STATUS OR BENEFIT.**

---

| RECEIPT NUMBER<br>SRC-14-900-81806 | | CASE TYPE I140 IMMIGRANT PETITION FOR ALIEN WORKER |
|---|---|---|
| RECEIPT DATE<br>December 11, 2013 | PRIORITY DATE<br>December 10, 2013 | PETITIONER<br>ADAMS, NICHOLAS |
| NOTICE DATE<br>March 2, 2016 | PAGE<br>1 of 1 | BENEFICIARY<br>ADAMS, NICHOLAS |
| NICHOLAS ADAMS<br>C/O NICK ADAMS<br><br>AUSTRALIA | | Notice Type: |

This is to advise you that we have reaffirmed our previous decision on the above application or petition which the Department of State had previously returned for review. We have forwarded the case back to the Department of State for action.

Section: Although this application/petition has been approved, USCIS and the U.S. Department of Homeland Security reserve the right to verify the information submitted in this application, petition and/or supporting documentation to ensure conformity with applicable laws, rules, regulations, and other activities. Methods used for verifying information may include, but are not limited to, the review of public information and records, contact by correspondence, the internet, or telephone, and site inspections of businesses and residences. Information obtained during the course of verification will be used to determine whether revocation, rescission, and/or removal proceedings are appropriate. Applicants, petitioners, and representatives of record will be provided an opportunity to address derogatory information before any formal proceeding is initiated.

Please see the additional information on the back. You will be notified separately about any other cases you filed.
USCIS
TEXAS SERVICE CENTER
P O BOX 851488 - DEPT A
MESQUITE   TX   75185-1488
Customer Service Telephone: (800) 375-5283

If this is an interview or biometrics appointment notice, please see the back of this notice for important information.          Form I-797C  07/11/14 Y

---

*It's official. The State Department gets slapped down. USCIS re-affirms my petition, proving that it should never have been sent back in the first place.*

★

My trip continues.

From DC, I travel victoriously back to my soon-to-be home state of Texas, and then from there to Atlanta, Charleston, and finally, back to and all over Texas.

After 78 days, it's time to fly back to Australia.

My career is back on track. I've recovered my mojo. I'm pumped for the opportunities already in place for the upcoming summer. I'm going to be an American—it's once more no longer in doubt.

Mission accomplished.

I board the Qantas A380 at DFW, and am suddenly hit by a wave of fatigue.

It's time to rest.

★

But I have never been one to rest too long.

Five days back, and I get wind of an incredible special that Qantas is running on the Sydney to Dallas route for dates in June.

Less than A$1,000 per person, return.

I know I have to be in Dallas for June 12.

Meanwhile, my parents have indicated that they want to both come to the DFW area and scope out the rental market, and help set me up for my new life.

So, all three of us book our flights together. It will be my father's first trip to America.

June 9 is the day. They'll stay for two weeks; I had a return ticket close to the 90-day threshold permitted for tourists, but I knew I was never going to stay that long—as I would likely be called for my Consulate interview way before then, and would fly back. With any luck, the interview might even happen before June 9, and then it'll be the trip where I immigrate.

It's April 17. Let's see what happens in the next seven weeks. We have lots to plan.

★

Ten days later, I get sensational news.

The IRS has granted FLAG—The Foundation for Liberty and American Greatness—its 501(c)(3) status, a massive step for its future. We're now a tax-exempt organization—all donations are entirely tax deductible.

We're on. My future is coming together.

★

Over May, I get all my affairs in order.

FLAG—my 501(c)(3) organization—to me, what Apple was to Steve Jobs, is occupying much of my time. I can barely wait to throw myself into our work.

I organize our letterhead, our website, our presentation folders, our first brochure, our business cards, and our first retractable banner. Meanwhile, mom and dad are perusing the Internet, taking note of certain apartment prospects and lining up appointments for us to see the places in person.

I line up, with fury, as many speaking engagements and donor opportunities as I can. I am working at full capacity—burning the candle at both ends—18-hour days.

In addition to this, on the counsel of The Wolf and my dad, I decide to renew my passport. It's got 11 months left on it, but really you shouldn't travel within 6 months of expiry, and the immigrant visa that I was going to receive from the Consulate would only be attached to a passport that had eight months validity. Again, I would be okay, but given I had some free time, and it was simply a matter of filling in a renewal form at the local post office, I went ahead and renewed it. Besides, if I didn't do it now, and I left it, then I'd have to renew it in America next year, which would mean going to the Consulate in New York and doing it there.

All the while, I patiently wait to hear from the US Consulate, with a date for interview. Nothing yet.

★

Late at night on June 8, our suitcases are almost packed.

Our hotel, airport parking, rental car, and itinerary have been arranged.

The big Turning Point USA Young Women's Leadership Summit is on in Dallas from June 12–15. This is huge for me, and for FLAG. Turning Point USA has been a big help to FLAG, and continues to be. I can't wait.

Not to mention, this is a special trip—with the whole family together in America for the first time.

I did a last minute check of items—and then it dawned on me that my existing ESTA (the visa waiver program that tourists from Australia travel on) was linked to my old passport. *Would they automatically link up,* I wondered. I did some quick research on the official site, and found that if your passport details had changed, you needed to get a new ESTA (which is simply an online application that takes five minutes).

So, I did. I paid my fourteen dollars, and applied.

My approval, as always, was instant.

★

June 9.

We load all our luggage in the car. The day couldn't have started any better.

The run to the airport was clear. Then we got the best parking spot imaginable at the airport parking. The airport itself seemed astonishingly empty.

There was no line at the Qantas check-in. We landed an extraordinarily friendly Qantas representative at our check-in counter. She even gave us better seats than the ones we had (and we already had good seats!).

She asked for our passports. We handed them over.

"Ah," she said. "Nick, did you forget to do your ESTA? Mom and Dad are good, but your ESTA is not showing."

"No," I said. "I've got my ESTA."

"When did you apply?" she asked?

"Last night," I responded.

"Mmm, that's strange," she says. "Should be in the system then. It goes in right away. Do you have a copy - can I see it?"

"Sure," I said, showing her. Her brows furrow.

Manually, while looking at my approved ESTA document, she re-entered in the information.

She looked up at the three of us.

"Look, I'm really sorry, but the computer is not accepting Nick's ESTA. I've never come across this before."

*Yeah,* I thought to myself, *been a lot of that going around.*

"I have to go and see my Supervisor and see if she can help."

★

Twenty-five minutes go by.

My mom has gone to take a seat with the hand luggage close by.

My dad and I wait at the counter, our sea of suitcases at our feet. It's taking much too long. There's definitely something up.

Now a line of other passengers has built behind the rope.

We're at 30 minutes.

★

The nice Qantas lady has returned with her Supervisor.

Their expressions belie several emotions: apologetic, wary, perplexed, and suspicious.

The Supervisor informs me that she has just called the Department of Homeland Security in America, and had been told that my ESTA had been denied, that I would not be permitted to enter the United States under the ESTA program, and that the only way I could travel to the US was to "make an appointment to get a paper visa from the Consulate."

"I asked them for the reason," she continues. "They didn't like me asking. They refused to provide it."

"But I have an approved ESTA," I protest. "I have it here; I can show you."

"Yes," she says, "but it has been revoked. It's no longer been approved. Everyone who applies for an ESTA is immediately granted approval, but then there is a silent second wave of scrutiny, not known to the public, done by DHS. And you were flagged," she explains regretfully. "If you logged on now, it will show that your ESTA has been denied."

★

I am shell-shocked.

"You appear to be on a no-fly list. Do you have any idea why this could be? Are you of Middle Eastern background? Have you visited the Middle East recently? Is this your first time to America, or have you been there before? Have you ever been convicted of a crime? Even as a juvenile?" The questions come thick and fast, but they weren't accusing. It was genuine curiosity to get to the bottom of something.

"I have been to the US 17 times on an ESTA in the last 7 years, most recently just a few months ago. No, I have no Middle Eastern background, nor have I ever visited the Middle East. I'm a patriot, and I have never even been arrested, or had any trouble with the law. I have no idea why I would be on a no-fly list," I explain. "None of this makes any sense," I complain. "In fact," I say, "I will be immigrating to the US soon—my Green Card petition has been approved, and I am just waiting for my interview at the Consulate."

They just look at me.

It's true, I want to say.

Well, Mr. Adams, we are really sorry, but you won't be able to travel today.

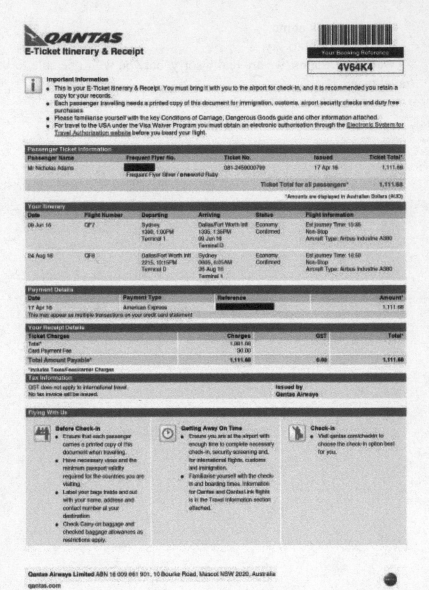

*The flight my parents and I were booked on; turned away at the airport. A day I will never forget.*

★

ESTA Application

Page 1 of 2

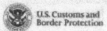 Official Website of the Department of Homeland Security

**U.S. Customs and Border Protection**

## AUTHORIZATION APPROVED

Your travel authorization has been approved and you are authorized to travel to the United States under the Visa Waiver Program. This does not guarantee admission to the United States; a Customs and Border Protection (CBP) officer at a port of entry will have the final determination.

If necessary, you can update the following information on an approved authorization: address while in the United States and e-mail address. To access your travel authorization, you will be required to provide your application number, Passport number, and birth date. If you need to change any other information on the form, you must apply for a new travel authorization.

## PAYMENT RECEIPT

You have successfully submitted payment for the application listed below. A request by the cardholder to the bank for a refund of fees will result in an automatic denial of the application. Please print this page for your personal records.

| NAME | DATE OF BIRTH | APPLICATION NUMBER | PASSPORT NUMBER | STATUS | EXPIRES |
|------|---------------|--------------------|-----------------| -------|---------|
| NICHOLAS ADAMS | Sep 5, 1984 | R1R6R67BRBC2A7KA | ▮▮▮▮▮ | Authorization Approved | Jun 8, 2018 |

### PAYMENT SUMMARY

| | |
|---|---|
| PAYMENT RECEIVED: | US $14.00 |
| PAYMENT DATE: | June 8, 2016 7:27:29 AM |
| PAYMENT TRACKING CODE: | 356408 |

To begin planning your trip to the United States today, please visit DiscoverAmerica.com the Official Travel and Tourism website of the United States.

U.S. Customs and Border Protection (CBP) has developed a new program called Automated Passport Control (APC) that expedites the entry process for eligible Visa Waiver Program international travelers by providing an automated process through CBP's Primary Inspection area. To learn more about APC and participating airports following this link: http://www.cbp.gov/travel/us-citizens/automated-passport-control-apc

**DHS RECOMMENDS YOU PRINT THIS SCREEN FOR YOUR RECORDS.**

Have a nice trip. Welcome to the United States.

file:///C:/Users/Administrator.LCC-12/Downloads/Nick%20ESTA%20Approval%20(... 24/07/2016

*The approved ESTA, June 8.*

Official Website of the Department of Homeland Security

 **U.S. Customs and Border Protection**

 Electronic System for Travel Authorization

## TRAVEL NOT AUTHORIZED

You are not authorized to travel to the United States under the Visa Waiver Program. You may be able to obtain a visa from the Department of State for your travel. Please visit the United States Department of State website at http://www.travel.state.gov/ for additional information about applying for a visa.

## PAYMENT RECEIPT

You have successfully submitted payment for the application listed below. A request by the cardholder to the bank for a refund of fees will result in an automatic denial of the application. Please print this page for your personal records.

| NAME | DATE OF BIRTH | APPLICATION NUMBER | PASSPORT NUMBER | STATUS | EXPIRES |
|------|---------------|--------------------|-----------------|--------|---------|
| NICHOLAS ADAMS | Sep 5, 1984 | R1R6R67BRBC2A7KA | ███ | Travel Not Authorized | N/A |

## PAYMENT SUMMARY

| | |
|---|---|
| **PAYMENT RECEIVED:** | US $14.00 |
| **PAYMENT DATE:** | June 8, 2016 7:27:29 AM |
| **PAYMENT TRACKING CODE:** | 356498 |

**DHS RECOMMENDS YOU PRINT THIS SCREEN FOR YOUR RECORDS**

Paperwork Reduction Act. An agency may not conduct or sponsor an information collection and a person is not required to respond to this information unless it displays a current valid OMB control number and an expiration date. The control number for this collection is 1651-0111. The estimated average time to complete this application is 22 minutes. If you have any comments regarding this burden estimate you can write to U.S. Customs and Border Protection, Office of Regulations and Rulings, 90 K Street, NE, 10th Floor, Washington DC 20229. Expiration Sep 30, 2016.

The ESTA logo is a registered trademark of the U.S. Department of Homeland Security. Its use, without permission, is unauthorized and in violation of trademark law. For more information, or to request the use of the logo, please go to help.cbp.gov and submit a request by clicking on "Ask a Question." When selecting the Product (under Additional Information) use "ESTA" and the sub-product "Logo Assistance" to expedite handling of your request.

file:///C:/Users/Administrator.LCC-12/Downloads/Nick%20ESTA%20Denied%20(1)...   24/07/2016

*Denied ESTA, June 9. Am I on a no-fly list?*

My mother is crying. My father yells at me to call the US Consulate. I explain you can't speak to anybody there. It's all automated with information.

We are sitting in chairs at the airport, not far from where everything had just gone down.

We are embarrassed. Distressed. Speechless. Shell-shocked. Angry.

I fight back tears.

★

It's pandemonium.

My dad paces around on his cell phone, trying to reach the airport parking company to see if he can get a refund on the two weeks upfront parking he has already paid.

I desperately try to reach the US Consulate in Sydney, and the US Embassy in Canberra. I try and call The Wolf.

None of us traveled that day.

★

The car ride home is excruciating.

It is mostly silence, punctuated by the odd call to the hotel or rental car company to cancel our reservations.

My mind races.

What has just happened?

How could I not be permitted to travel to the United States? How on earth could it be possible that I'm on a no-fly list? I have an approved Green Card petition pending, for heaven sakes. My mind swirls.

All the feelings of September through November 2015 come flooding back to me. The shock. The despair. The uncertainty. The helplessness. Déjà vu.

And then, the worst thing of all. Letting down people, cancelling events, and explaining what has happened.

★

Thirty events. That's the number of events I have to cancel. Not to mention the number of people who have made special travel arrangements either to support me, or planned to attend an event. I make arrangements for people to collect packages that await me at various hotels. An account of what happened at the airport needs to be written and sent to key people too.

With a steadfastness and willpower that surprised me, for three hours straight, I send fifty-six emails.

Once done, I sit in my office all alone. My head instinctively hangs, and I shake it.

I think about the reaction to the news. There will be lots of support: "don't worry about it," "we'll reschedule," and "hang in there."

People won't say it to me, because they are too nice, but I know human nature too well. Now that this has happened a second time, people are going to begin to think there is a problem with me. It's a normal reaction. I can't blame them.

My reputation has taken an incredible hit.

Right now, I hate my life. I hate the system. I hate my predicament.

I turn to God and pray.

★

By the next morning, my disbelief and shock has turned to anger.

I am ready for war.

I am convinced that the Consulate in Sydney has had something to do with me not being able to travel to the United States. *But, wait,* I think to myself, *the Consulate is under the State Department, and this ESTA stuff is dealt with by DHS. Two different departments.* No, it must be. What else can it be?

Here's my theory: I believe the Sydney Consulate is sore about their recommendation not being accepted by USCIS, and that I used my trip to America earlier this year to mobilize political support for my application and further my extraordinary ability case. Once they realized what I had done, they stepped in to make sure that traveling to the US to defend myself and create public awareness of my application would not be possible. They made the call to DHS and got me "flagged."

The Wolf agrees with my likely assessment of Consular involvement, and says the "block is disturbing." So do others.

I am ready to tear the collective hind legs off a herd of antelopes.

I steady myself for another round of political lobbying, and realize that my American Dream is once more far in the distance.

★

If I'm right with my suspicions, then I'm in for a very hard time by the Consulate when I go up there for another interview, if they even acknowledge the existence of my application.

This will be a huge test. I am not looking forward to the interview. It's just one on one. I can't bring a witness or an observer. What happens if they just fabricate what happens during the course of the interview?

If they've already intervened to get me on a no-fly list, who knows what they are capable of?

In fact, maybe they have engineered all this. I remembered one of the very first questions The Wolf ever asked me was if I had ever been denied entry to the United States. "Of course not," I had responded, almost indignantly.

"That's good, because that would complicate things," had been his calm response.

Did the Consulate assume I would try to travel, based on past history and the fact that I still hadn't received notice for a new interview, and know that I would be stopped, therefore being able to suggest I had been denied entry? Was this their new strategy with my application? Did I just give them the opportunity they were looking for? The gift they were waiting for?

Had I been set up?

★

It's the deadliest terrorist attack since 9-11. The deadliest mass shooting in American history.

I watch in disbelief as Fox News reports the Orlando terror at Pulse, a gay nightclub.

I am distraught at the loss of innocent life, the pain the families involved must feel, and I am angry that this keeps happening.

It's time to understand that Islam is not compatible with the American value system, and that we are at war with radical Islamic terrorism.

I feel America needs me, my voice, my strength, and patriotism now more than ever.

But again, all I can do is look on concerned from the sidelines.

★

For the last few days, I have been furious.

Then I hear from Patricia Sykes of Senator Graham's office.

She hadn't been in to the office on Friday, and responded to me first thing Monday morning. *My Monday night.*

Her email hit me right between the eyes.

Turns out it had nothing to do with the Consulate. I had been flagged as an intending immigrant, and "intending immigrants" can't travel to America on an ESTA (as a tourist). I could apply for a B1 or B2 non-immigrant visa through the Sydney Consulate, and would just need to provide compelling reasons that I would return to my home country. My upcoming interview at the Consulate would have satisfied that.

★

I am relieved. We are relieved.

I had never been on a no-fly list. I had never technically been denied entry at a US port.

The best part of the news is that there is no persecution from the Consulate, and I am still on track for the Green Card.

Given that I expect my interview to happen within the next few weeks, there is no point applying for a B1 or B2 visa.

Now the message from the Department of Homeland Security as relayed by the Qantas supervisor makes sense: *"you are not permitted to enter the United States under the ESTA program, and the only way you could travel to the US was to make an appointment to get a paper visa from the Consulate."*

The Wolf's cautions about 'intending immigrants" not being able to enter the US and a possible "flag," now made sense too. He had been right all along!!

I feel very sheepish. I was wrong. It is unlike me to be conspiratorial, but what else was I to think? This is the climate that the individual in the US Consulate in Sydney brought to my application with his rare and unwarranted action—now I operate in a climate of distrust, fear, and concern.

Amidst all of this, I still have a burning question.

Why was I flagged now, but not before? I have been an "intending immigrant" by the definition of USCIS since December 2014. Since then, I've been to America three times. What was different then?

And then the timeline dawned on me.

ESTAs are good for two years.

- I got an ESTA in November 2014, for my November– December trip.
- A month later, in December 2014, they approved my Green Card petition.
- I travelled in April 2015, and June–July 2015.

- Then all hell broke loose in September 2015 with the Consulate.
- After a few months of pain, I took the gamble and travelled between January–April 2016.

But then I had prudently renewed my passport in May 2016, without realizing that the very action invalidates your current ESTA and requires you to get a new one.

This time when I applied for a new ESTA, the DHS did have me flagged. As luck had it, my previous ESTA had been granted one month before my Green Card petition was originally approved, which meant that there was no flag on it, and why I had no problem traveling to the US. "Flags" don't go on existing ESTAs (the dots don't get connected); only new applications for one trigger them.

I had no idea about any of this. After having been able to travel at will, I always assumed the ESTA would be open to me. The system doesn't make sense. It's a shambles. If you have an approved Green Card petition and then have to wait six to nine months before your immigrant visa interview at a Consulate in your home country, are you supposed to suspend life for that period of time? Why can't you go to America during that time to continue your work periodically, or begin to plan for your new life? If you are in America, you need to return to your country to conduct your US Consulate interview, anyway. So, how is immigrant intent even applicable before that point? The system needs a complete overhaul.

★

Here's the rub.

This is the part that hurts.

My old ESTA, with the old passport number, was valid until November 2016.

If I had not been so overly prudent about renewing my passport, which still had eleven months validity at the time, I would be in America right now on that same trusty ESTA.

As my friend John Rogitz told me today, ". . . 99.9% of the time, being proactive like you were is a positive thing. You just ran into the other 0.1% in one hell of a special and rare circumstance, unfortunately encountered as it was."

★

But despite this, relief soon turns to self-flagellation.

I had screwed up. Badly. The magnitude of it has hit me.

And it was all on me. It is one thing to be able to have someone to pin the blame on. It's another thing entirely when you have nobody else to blame but you.

But can you screw up without knowing you are screwing up? What a colossal, innocent debacle.

Try as I might, I try and cook it up every which way in my own mind for it to sit more comfortably, but I just can't. If I thought I was embarrassed then, now I am positively mortified.

The dozens of missed opportunities, the hundreds of people I let down, the events I had to cancel, the collective hit all of these things have on my reputation, the unforgettable and indelible scenes at the airport for my parents . . . I am just sick to my stomach.

"Son," my father says, "don't worry about it. Sometimes in life, you can make a mistake without knowing it's a mistake. As Tony Abbott says," he reminds me, "'Shit happens.'"

Soon, you'll be an immigrant and all of this will be a distant memory.

★

A fortnight passes, and I am in a holding pattern.

We await the email from the US Consulate in Sydney, providing notification of an interview date.

★

Friday, June 23.

Brexit.

It's early Friday afternoon in Australia when the result has become clear. The United Kingdom finally takes their country back, pulling off an incredible victory for patriotism and common sense, seen by few as possible.

Finally, it seems, the snapback worldwide has started against political correctness and the out-of-touch elites who thrust it upon us. As Nigel Farage said, "This is a victory for ordinary people, for good people, for decent people."

They are exactly the type of Americans I envision FLAG representing.

I am greatly encouraged. The world has finally taken a step in the right direction.

★

Sunday, June 26.

My dad, 59, is extremely unwell, and in great pain.

My mom urgently sends me out to get some aspirin.

For the last few days, he has experienced back, shoulder, and chest pains. With the help of Dr. Google, we diagnose it as unstable angina.

It's time to see the doctor and cardiologist.

★

Later that night, I'm alarmed to find a handwritten note leaving instructions and bank passwords.

He seems to think his time is up, or very close.

This is killing me.

★

Monday, June 27.

We get a referral from our family physician, and with some pushing, I manage to secure an appointment with a local cardiologist that afternoon.

The news is not good, but nothing can be known for certain until an angiogram is performed in the hospital. For the time being, he needs to add an impressive repertoire of three heart tablets to his daily diet.

I look at him as we drive to the drugstore. The color has drained from his skin.

There is clearly something wrong with his heart, which is bad news, any way you crack it up.

He's my hero and the strongest man I know. This is rough.

Tuesday, June 28.

At 1:03pm, I get an email!

*Dear Mr. Adams,*

*I am writing in regard to your immigrant visa application for which you had been interviewed on September 22, 2015. We have been authorized to continue processing your application, therefore, we need you to mail into our office the following documents before September 21, 2016. A new interview will be required if your visa is not issued before September 21, 2016.*

## *DOCUMENTS REQUIRED:*

*Valid passport*

*One recent passport sized photograph*

*Original and one photocopy of your birth certificate with name change included*

*Original Australian police certificate (need to submit an updated copy as the previous one expired on January 27, 2016)*

*Evidence of your own assets and/or U.S. job offer*

*Updated medical report (yours had expired on February 29, 2016)*

*One 5kg self-addressed express post envelope.*

*Upon receipt of your documents we will continue processing your application to conclusion. Alternatively, should any additional information be required, we will contact you via email.*

Not even an interview!!!

Just send in your documents!!! How good is this?! This is even better than I could have hoped for.

I'm with my dad when I get the email. As I read it aloud to him, his eyes water, and his voice chokes.

They've forgotten to include a mailing address. *Can you believe it?*

I write to them, asking for it. They respond soon afterward.

They mustn't send many emails like this out, obviously.

I visit the family physician again. Between my father and me, he must be sick of us this week.

In preparation for the medical exam, I get a blood test, and establish I need a booster for a couple of the vaccines I received last year.

And another flu shot.

I get it done.

Talk about déjà vu.

★

It's Monday, July 4, an ordinary day in Australia.

Today I must redo my medical exam with the same doctor as 11 months earlier—and pay him another $457.

My dad accompanies me to my medical exam, and can't wipe the scowl from his face. Me having to do this all again just infuriates him no end. Not for the first time that hour, he curses the official from the US Consulate, in rather unparliamentary language. I do too.

Dr Waks is one of only three Australian physicians on the US government's payroll certified to conduct these examinations. Dr. Waks is close to ninety, but still going strong in his Sydney office. He expresses surprise at having to see me again. I give him the basics. He has been working for the US Consulate for a long time, and tells me he has never heard or seen a case like mine. The only time where he has seen an applicant a second time is when the Consulate discovered their criminal record, and that reveals they had been dishonest during the medical exam with Dr. Waks. "Sounds like a personality clash with this guy at the Consulate," he says wisely. "Oh well, you'll just have to wear it, mate."

★

I am a healthy 31-year old boy, and pass the medical with flying colors.

★

On Wednesday, July 6, I submit all my documentation in an Express Post envelope, via registered mail.

That's it.

Now, we wait.

My father tells me he just wants to be well enough to get to America to help set me up. He said he just hopes to make it there once, set me up there and then come home and "rest."

I'm breaking up inside.

I could cry.

★

The last three days have been agony.

Seeing my father in such pain kills me. He is a proud man, and stubbornly refuses to go to the hospital, despite our insistence. He hates the place.

It's 4:42am now, and I can't sleep. My own heart is racing. The light is on in the kitchen, so I know he is up again, because he can't sleep. He hasn't really slept in a week. His pain seems to come most when he lies down.

During one or two of these attacks, I have even witnessed him using a special pump spray that he sprays under his tongue.

Worse still, when he feels an attack coming on, he leaves the room, because he doesn't want me to see it. I, of course, want to be present every waking minute, phone in hand, ready to call an ambulance.

I reluctantly go to sleep every night, terrified I am going to be woken by my mother with awful news.

★

At 7:30am on Friday morning, my father reports to the hospital, accompanied by his concerned spouse and child. It is time for him to have his angiogram.

Two and a half hours later, I get terrible news.
My father has three blocked arteries, and can't come home.

As I drive home with my mother, we hear over the radio the news of the killing of five police officers in Dallas and the injuring of multiple others, at the end of a Black Lives Matter protest.

My own heart has much reason to cry tonight.

It weeps for my father, the families of those brave officers that perished protecting the public, and the country I love.

My father was born with an atrial septal defect (ASD), or a hole in his heart, but it was undiagnosed until he was 36. He had open heart surgery in September 1998, which fixed the problem. But up until he was 40, his heart was operating at twice the pace of a normal person, so he already has the heart of a 75 year old.

In the last few years, he has suffered from what many middle-aged men have—diabetes and high blood pressure. It has all caught up with him.

But the major point here is—he's already been opened up once, and I know he vows he will never let it happen again. It took him a year to recover then, and he was just forty. No way will he put himself through that again.

I blame myself.

This is all stress-related, I thought. This is that Consular official's legacy, I think angrily.

One man in one office on one day has caused all our lives to go into a tailspin. And for what? Because he didn't like my politics? He didn't like what I stood for? He didn't like comments I had made in the media? He didn't want a conservative commentator immigrating to the US? He didn't want my presence assisting Republicans in an election year?

★

Bypass surgery is what the doctors at first urge.

"No," my father responds resolutely. "Stents only."

★

While in the hospital, the pain stops as the medication changes.

At least, I can sleep again. And so can he.

Every day as I come in to visit, and every night as I arrive back home, his first question always is: "Did you check the mail—did it arrive?"

"Not yet, Dad," I say.

"It will come soon," he says, "and then we're all going for a trip to America, and I'm going to enjoy a huge Texas steak."

On these occasions, I'm happy the cardiologists aren't around to hear a heart patient talk about steak—it may be enough to cause their own hearts to stop!

★

Late Monday night, the 11th of July, we receive the wonderful news. They can do stents—they don't need to do the bypass surgery.

That night I look at the sky and its abundant stars, and thank God profusely.

★

On Tuesday, the 12th of July, my father had stents successfully inserted.

By Wednesday afternoon, he's back home.

Now, all that remains is the immigrant visa package from the US Consulate.

Visas typically take 5–7 business days to issue.

But since when has the government ever been on time?

★

Thursday comes, and goes.

I ask Senator Graham's office to request that the issuing of my visa be issued as a top priority, given the history of the application. They do so.

Friday comes, and goes. Again, I watch in abject horror as the reports begin to flow in from Nice about a terror attack on Bastille Day, where a truck was used as a tank to run over scores of people.

*Not again.* This must stop. We must stand up for Christianity, defend our heritage, and protect the West.

★

The weekend comes, and goes. Surely it will arrive on Monday.

★

Monday comes, and goes.

Vice President Joe Biden is in Sydney—I guess that, probably, had them busy today.

★

Tuesday, July 19, 2016.

I wake to see the first night of the Republican National Convention in Cleveland, Ohio.

Virtually everyone I know—at Fox, CNN, the conservative movement, and in Republican Party circles—is there.

All my life, I have wanted to attend a Republican National Convention. And this year, I would have been speaking there too.

Try as I might, I can't escape it. It's all over my Facebook, all over Fox News, and even all over Australian TV.

I feel gutted.

I try to remind myself, for what feels like the millionth time, of God's plan, and that His timing is perfect.

★

Four hours later, at 10:50am, I get an email.

The subject line? *Notice of approved, issued and mailed immigrant visas.*

The first two lines? *Dear Visa Applicant, We are pleased to advise that your visa has been issued today!*

★

It's over. It's finally over. I have an Extraordinary Ability Green Card.

The Wolf says he and the team are thrilled and delighted.

It has taken 19 months since my Green Card petition was first approved.

Three and a half years since I engaged The Wolf.

More than four years since I first engaged an immigration attorney.

And 7 years since I first visited an immigration attorney.

★

My mother cries with relief.

My father cries with relief.

We have been to hell and back.

I celebrate with an ice cream.

★

I wait with eager anticipation on Wednesday for my visa, and its accompanying package.

It doesn't arrive.

*That's strange,* I think, *because one of the things they asked me to include was an Express Post envelope. That just takes 24 hours.*

Using the tracking number from the Express Post envelope, I enter it in to the Australia Post system. It shows no action.

I've done this at least ten times today.

★

It still hasn't arrived on Thursday.

I send an email:

*Dear Sir/Madam,*

*I received an email on Tuesday morning from your office, indicating that my immigrant visa had been approved, issued, and mailed.*

*I am worried that I haven't received it yet. Express Post should be overnight. That means I should have received it yesterday or this morning.*

*Could you please confirm that my passport/visa has been mailed? If not, can you tell me when? Or alternatively, is it possible for me to come and pick up my package, please?*

*Your quick response would be greatly appreciated.*

*Sincerely,*

*Nick Adams*

I check the status of the tracking number every couple of hours.
Nothing. This can't be happening, can it?
I mean, really and truly.
Finally, 8 hours later, I get an email.

*Dear Mr. Adams,*

*Thank you for your email.*

*Our office actually received your package back today from our mail room as being overweight. We can either repackage this and mail it out or you may collect from our office tomorrow between 10am and noon or Monday at 2.30pm.*

*Please reply to advise what you prefer to do so we may either mail this out or alert our guards that you will be collecting.*

*Thank you*

***Immigrant Visa Unit (AT)***
***U.S. Consulate General, Sydney***

*See you there at 10am tomorrow*, I write back.
   Imagine if I hadn't written to them. Were they even going to tell me? No apology—just arrogance—and these are the people that represent America abroad.
   All I can do is shake my head.

★

I pick the package up.
   It is in my hands.

As I walk through Martin Place, Sydney's version of Times Square, holding the 17-pound package that would enable me to enter America to accept my Green Card, tears stream down my face.

It dawns on me.

I had taken on the State Department under President Obama, and won.

Again, I had defied the odds.

My prize?

Becoming what I had been born to be.

An American.

# EPILOGUE

There is much I want to say.

Much I think the American people must know.

I want you to know what some honest and good people go through to become Americans.

I know that unless you have personally experienced or been affected by the immigration process it is likely an area you know little about. For example, despite having been an Australian for almost 32 years, I have no idea about the legal immigration process to Australia.

For centuries, books have been written in an attempt to share discoveries and knowledge. Sometimes those books make such an impact that they change the way the world thinks about things. I want this book to be one of them. I want it to herald a widespread shake-up of the immigration system in America. I don't want others to experience what I did.

Why is the legal immigration process so tough, but illegal immigration so easy? Why does the government insist on seeing evidence of a legal immigrant's ability to sustain themselves lest they be a burden on the government (after having just spent $40,000 on legal and filing fees just to have the privilege of being asked), but have no interest and pay no attention to the substantial drain that is illegal immigration?

Why does it take years to do it the right way but it is almost immediate to do it the wrong way? Why is there such secrecy in details of the legal process, yet illegals cross in plain view of

Americans? Why is it I must carry a CD proving I do not have tuberculosis in case I'm asked for it by a border official at the time of receiving my Green Card, but when an illegal walks into Texas, we don't know what diseases their body carries?

If you're an illegal and crossed the Rio Grande, you get free food stamps, health insurance, don't have to pay taxes and are spoiled by every benefit from state and federal government.

If you're a Syrian coming to America, you're undocumented, unvetted, and welcome.

As one friend put it to me in an email:

*These guys want to bring in the riff raff from the Middle East, who have sworn to destroy America one way or the other, and they allow them to come in by the thousands, while people we want to come in to America can't get through all the red tape. We make it easy for the worst to come here and impossible for the best.*

Or as another put it:

*You had three strikes against you: you were a Christian, a patriot and conservative.*

But if you obey the law, you get kicked in the teeth. Repeatedly.

Even at the very end, it continued. Once I received my immigrant visa, I had to pay a final immigrant fee of $165. In the overall scheme of things, this is not a large amount. However, it is not insignificant, particularly when Afghani and Iraqi immigrants are exempt.

How is any of this fair? Or reasonable? Or in accordance with the Constitution or the American ethos?

You've read my story, and shared in the ups and the downs. The triumphs and the failures. The ecstasy and the supreme disappointment. It is a phenomenal story of human endurance.

All my life, I have fought.

At 16 months when I was diagnosed with Stage IV cancer, and given just a 5 percent chance of life, I fought for three years, and won.

Throughout high school, I fought the establishment, and despite never being one of the favored students, left having topped the school in three of the four final subjects.

At 19, I fought the Left, and won a spot in local government. Against all odds, I was elected to Deputy Mayor, making history as the youngest ever elected to that role.

At university, I fought the Left in faculty, and won.

Fighting has always come naturally because I love life. I want to live too much. My ambition—my hunger for success and achievement—has always seen me through.

As a conservative young upstart who refused to worship at the altar of political correctness in a country of conformity, it was permissible to degrade, humiliate and vilify me. My own conservative party was full of little totalitarians doing everything they could do to silence me. It was the cruellest, non-criminal behavior imaginable.

So, I did not come to my immigration situation as a wide-eyed novice. I came as a seasoned veteran of leftist and establishment oppression.

But this still did not prepare me for the Consular official and the others who must have supported him.

This was not a fair fight.

It was unwarranted, and evil. Arrogant and personal. Abusive and discriminatory.

This was political persecution, plain and simple.

By denying my immigrant visa when it was all but a formality, the Consular official acted arrogantly, without merit, and abused his position because he wanted to vilify an enemy of the Left.

It didn't matter to him how much money my family had spent on legal and filing fees. He disregarded what a future asset I would be for his country. He didn't care about the turmoil my family had to endure. All because he could not see past my politics.

For ten months, in the prime of my life, my career was stalled. My personal life put on hold. I almost ran out of money. Hundreds of opportunities were missed. This all coincided with the most exciting political and cultural election year imaginable. One of FLAG's founding Advisory Board members and close supporter, the wonderful former Senator from Colorado, and most recently President of Colorado Christian University, Bill Armstrong, never got to make a FLAG meeting, as he sadly passed as I waited for my second Consulate interview.

Friendships tested. Some people stayed the course; many didn't. Connections disappeared. Most put me in the "too hard" basket. I'm grateful to know which friends were fair-weather and which were all-weather. To the latter, I have only sincere admiration and immeasurable thanks. A special tap of the mitts to my friend John Rogitz, from San Diego.

Lifelong dreams like attending the Republican National Convention missed. My tireless work in getting on the radar of Fox News executives was for nothing.

In so many ways, I must begin again.

Hundreds, if not thousands, were let down by me over the course of this saga. I can never adequately apologize to those people. All I can do is promise you I will do my best to make it up to you.

It has been particularly painful to watch as contemporaries in my industry have been elevated well above their station, purely by virtue of being present and available.

As I think about the sum of this, it is just too much to bear sometimes.

This was one of the worst experiences of my life.

Someone, somewhere along the line, needs to be accountable for this.

This can't be allowed to happen this way, without consequences for those who are responsible for the decisions.

The face of America cannot be people like the individual at the Consulate I encountered. America must keep the bad people out, and let the good people in. In US Consulates and Embassies around the world, you need people who are going to be fair and reasonable, and have the best interests of America at heart.

During my trials, I heard firsthand the story of Paul, an Indian national who was working at a household-name multinational IT company on a HB-1 visa. He, too, had the approval of the USCIS, but suffered at the hands of a Consular Official in New Delhi. A Senator's office got involved, at the request of the multinational company for which he was working, but while this intervention helped him get a second visit to the Consulate, it earned him the ire of the Consular official, with the latter asking: "What makes you so special I am getting calls about you?"

Paul never again heard from the Consulate, the multinational lost patience, and Paul had no money to fight the case or engage an attorney. He was forced to sell all his belongings in America from India, and started a new life with his young family in Australia. This was four years ago. When Paul enters his case number and logs in today, the system still shows his application to still be "Under Consular Review."

This type of behavior is outrageous, unacceptable, and un-American. It must end now.

For a progressive world addicted to the virtue of "transparency," there is absolutely none in the legal immigration process.

I want to be the voice for those who have suffered already, and those who would love to become great patriots of America but hear of the suffering and tumult involved, and never start the process.

I implore you, America, to fix your system because it is destroying careers, destroying families, destroying people's finances, and destroying's people's health.

Anti-Americanism has no place in our world, but if those who would harbor such bigotry had only ever dealt with an "American" like I had to, who could blame them?

Here I was a young man in love with America. Whose life has been dedicated to protecting America. My extraordinary ability was indisputable.

In the end, I had the rare honor of being deemed worthy of an Extraordinary Ability Green Card, *twice*. Not many people can say that!!

My immigrant visa should have been granted on September 22, 2015. It wasn't. Let me be clear: I hold only the US Consulate in Sydney responsible for this. Twice, the United States Citizenship and Immigration Service did their job, responsibly and fairly.

It is the US Consulate in Sydney that does not have America's back.

FLAG's first mission is to expose the actions of this Consular official.

Vice Consuls are impeachable by Congress.

On FlagUSA.org, there is a petition calling for the impeachment of this individual.

I encourage all of you to sign it.

I call on you to lobby your local Congressman and Senator so that an investigative Congressional hearing be held on Capitol Hill.

I will seek justice for my family and me.

I am a model American immigrant—precisely the type of person you would want in your country.

Becoming an American is a special privilege.

From the moment I got my Green Card or permanent residency, I became an American.

In five years' time, and not a day later (the law requires me to have lived in America for exactly five years), I will knock on the door of my local USCIS office, dressed in my best suit and one bought specifically for the occasion, ready for my naturalization ceremony. With enormous pride, I will recite the Oath of Allegiance, an oath I have memorized by heart already, and been practicing since I was a child. It will be the greatest day of my life.

I want to be clear.

It is important for me to acknowledge that I have come to America to be American. If I wanted to be Australian, I would have stayed in Australia. I acknowledge I am coming to America because she is a better country than the one I was born in. She offers more opportunity, more freedom, the American Dream, and, yes, less political correctness. The Constitution is the best political document ever written. The American value system is the greatest value system ever devised. The United States military is the greatest fighting force the world has ever seen and the strongest vehicle against evil ever.

I don't come to America to change it; I come to enhance it. I come to make, not take. Give, not receive.

Obviously, I speak English, but if I didn't, I would have learned, because this is the language of your country.

I cannot wait to fly the American flag outside my house. I will make sure the children I plan to have are experts on flag protocol and this nation's history, and are raised as proud Americans.

The United States of America is the greatest country in the world, and I am prepared to do everything I have to do to keep it that way. Your challenge is mine, and I will work as hard, if not harder, than anyone in overcoming America's threats and defeating its enemies.

Finally, let me say: I put my money where my mouth was. I chose America. I know I'm immigrating to America in difficult times. I know I'm coming at a time when many suggest America's best days are behind her. But I don't believe it. I'm immigrating to America because I still believe in America. I'm immigrating to America because I want America to be number one again. I want America to stop apologizing and start leading.

Always believe in America!

It's never too late.

America is special in that it is not just a country. Not just a geographical entity. Not merely a collection of fifty states. Not simply a stretch of land. It's an idea, an ideal, a concept, a notion. This is why in five thousand years of recorded human history, we have never seen another country like America. It's the best idea the world has ever had.

The only people capable of rejecting political correctness, of destroying it, are Americans. I can tell you that having been an outsider. I know it's hard to imagine it being worse than what it is, but trust me when I say: America is the last stand. Everyone else is too far gone. Your founding and your culture allow you to be different. American exceptionalism can crush political correctness, but at the moment, it's the other way around.

I know I am stronger because of this.

I know I am special because of this.

I know that what happened to me was part of God's plan. And I can predict FLAG's success in becoming an unstoppable cultural force and change agent in America, an antidote to the Left, precisely because of what I was forced to go through.

Despite all I have been through, I still believe in you, America. I still love you.

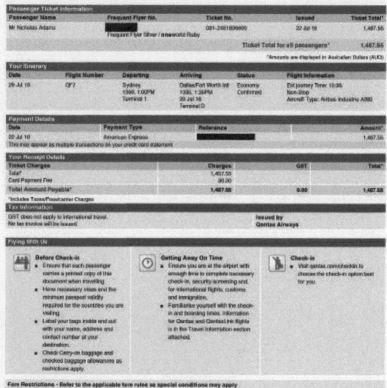

*July 29. A one way ticket to America.*

# SUPPORTING FLAG

**Dear Patriot,**

This year marks America's 240<sup>th</sup> birthday.

While a cause for great celebration, it is also a time for sober reflection.

History tells us the lifespan of great nations tends to be between 200 to 250 years. That puts America—the country, the idea, the value system—right in the "kill zone."

To ensure America reaches her third centennial in 2076, a feat few great nations achieve, Americans of all ages, colors, and creeds will need to answer the call with informed patriotism.

We must take decisive action now.

The situation is grave.

There is a war on America, and the enemies are no longer simply foreign; they are also domestic.

The national media. Teachers. Professors. Celebrities. The politically correct. Those with the loudest megaphones are drowning out truth and forcing America to whisper.

Their goal is simple, but transformative:

- Cripple American confidence.
- Question America's legitimacy.
- Diminish America on the world stage.
- Deny American exceptionalism.
- Make patriotic pride suspect.

- Create a self-loathing nation, unwilling to fight for itself, or what is right.

Their success cannot be disputed.

Patriotism is in decline, with just one-third of millennials believing the United States is the greatest country in the world. Younger generations are increasingly reluctant to express patriotism, and feel a belief in American exceptionalism is neither inclusive nor in keeping with the concept of "equality."

America's bravest have our back in the air, at sea and on land. But who has America's back in the culture? In classrooms? On television? In newspapers?

Who guards America's reputation? Who exposes anti-Americans? Who defends America's honor? Who makes the case for America? Who teaches our children what it means to be an American? About what it is that makes America special? About all that America has done for the world? And about what would happen were America not the world's leader?

FLAG—The Foundation for Liberty and American Greatness—does.

FLAG is not a think tank. We are a 501(c)(3) battle-tank, seeking to create a patriotic movement that will sweep across the country, effect fundamental generational change, and transform America and the world.

Our battlefield is the cultural battlefield—at home and abroad.

We're committed to stopping the defamation of the American people worldwide, and making American exceptionalism reach the hearts and minds of every child in this country. We understand the value of educating the public on patriotic principles to America's promise and future. We recognize we can no longer afford to allow America's cultural enemies to play unopposed. It's why FLAG serves as an educational organization and a rapid-response media team.

We are a voice for America, where there isn't one.

FLAG is new, but the work is a continuation. For the last seven years, I have traveled throughout America and the world, reinvigorating patriotism by educating audiences on American greatness from an "outsider's perspective." During the same time, I have aggressively countered anti-American hate and bias at every opportunity. I've done this writing books, giving speeches, and in the media.

The most precious treasure of any organization is its "brain trust." For FLAG's Advisory Council, I have assembled some of the finest conservative, experienced, and tactical minds in the country. Many have held leadership positions inside some of America's greatest organizations, including The Heritage Foundation, The Leadership Institute, Turning Point USA, and The Centennial Institute. These men all have a proven record of significantly promoting American exceptionalism and identifying and targeting anti-American values on campus, in the media and on the world stage.

We all stand ready to serve, under the new umbrella of FLAG.

But for us to achieve our goals and our vision, and implement the resources and programs required, we need your help.

Your support of FLAG is an investment in our children and an investment in the America they will inherit.

FLAG may have been founded by me. But if it only exists in my lifetime, its mission, and my work, will have failed in its ambition. FLAG must become an institution, recognized worldwide.

We must recommit to those principles that make our nation great. America can only be at her best when she is true to her founding, her values, and her promise.

We did not seek nor did we provoke this war on America. We did not expect nor did we invite this unforgivable assault on American values.

But we will neither run nor hide. America's time as the world's punching bag is up.

It's time for a new patriotic and conservative revolution. It's time to forge a new American generation that guarantees the American Dream for another 200 years.

No less than the entire world's health is at stake.

America must always be the rainbow in our clouds.

Join us today in leaving a legacy and making history. Visit www.flagusa.org, and make a donation.

Yours Faithfully,
Nick Adams
Founder & Executive Director,
Foundation for Liberty and American Greatness
(FLAG)

# ACKNOWLEDGEMENTS

Special thank you to the patriots in the following offices for their help, or preparedness to help:

- Office of Senator Lindsay Graham, particularly Patricia Sykes
- Office of Senator Tim Scott, particularly Danae Lara
- Office of Senator Cory Gardner, particularly Rebecca Rudder
- Office of Senator John McCain, particularly Ana Armendarez
- Office of Senator Jeff Sessions, particularly Jeff Sessions
- Office of Congressman Joe Barton, particularly Jodi Saegesser
- Office of Congressman Adam Kinzinger, particularly Bonnie Walsh
- Office of Congressman Steve Womack, particularly Janet Foster
- Office of Congressman Pete Sessions, particularly Flo Helton
- Office of Congressman Bill Flores, particularly Miranda Henderson
- Office of Congressman Scott Tipton, particularly Doug Fitzgerald
- Office of Congressman Ken Buck, particularly Erika Chaves

- Office of Congressman Mike Kelly, particularly Tom Qualtere
- Governor Tom Ridge
- Governor Rick Perry

# ABOUT THE AUTHOR

Nick Adams is the Founder and Executive Director of FLAG, The Foundation for Liberty and American Greatness (www.flagusa. org). He is an internationally renowned speaker, lecturer, author, and commentator. He is best known for his work in the field of American exceptionalism and is credited with fueling a resurgence in the idea worldwide. He is a Fellow of Colorado Christian University. He has spoken throughout America, Germany, South Korea, and the United Kingdom. He contributes to numerous media organizations and has received several state awards, including honorary citizenship, as well as being recognized for "extraordinary ability" by the U.S Government. Adams holds degrees in Media and Communications, Government and International Relations, Germanic Studies, and Education from the University of Sydney. In 2005, at the age of twenty-one, he was elected as the youngest deputy mayor in Australian history, a record he still holds to this day.